D0126319

Pq- Duw - 420

DECISIONS

JIM TRELIVING

DECISIONS

Making the Right Ones, Righting the Wrong Ones

Collins

Decisions
Copyright © 2012 by James Treliving Media Ltd.
All rights reserved.

Published by Collins, an imprint of HarperCollins Publishers Ltd

First edition

HarperCollins books may be purchased for educational, business, or sales
promotional use through our Special Markets Department.

HarperCollins Publishers Ltd
2 Bloor Street East, 20th Floor
Toronto, Ontario, Canada
M4W 1A8

www.harpercollins.ca

Library and Archives Canada Cataloguing in Publication

Treliving, Jim, 1941–
Decisions : making the right ones, righting the wrong ones / Jim
Treliving.

ISBN 978-1-44341-181-3

1. Decision making. 2. Problem solving. 3. Success in business.
I. Title.
HD30.23.T74 2012   658.4'03   C2012-903113-5

Printed and bound in the United States

RRD 9 8 7 6 5 4 3 2 1

This book is dedicated to my wife, Sandi, who's also my partner in life, and to my business partner, George Melville. I also devote it to my daughter, Cheryl; my son, Brad, and his wife, Julie; my granddaughters, Candace, Samantha, Ryann and Reese; my step-children, Katie and Dan; and my sisters, Joy and Pat, and their families. My family has always been my inspiration, but my parents, Ted and Mina Treliving, were the first to inspire me.

CONTENTS

*"Whenever you see a successful business,
someone once made a courageous decision."*
—Peter F. Drucker

INTRODUCTION

The Smallest Big Decision I Ever Made

What I remember most about that December night in 1966 was the cold. I was with a friend of mine, a city police officer named Don Spence. I was a 27-year-old RCMP officer newly transferred from Prince George, in northern BC, to Edmonton. That frigid night we were driving around, feeling a little restless after a busy night shift. Those are the times you don't want to go home right away without unwinding over a meal or you'll find it really hard to fall asleep. I had been a police officer for almost a decade by then, so I had my routines, and a late-night bite after a long shift was one of them.

"Feel like grabbing pizza, Jim?" Don asked close to midnight.

Why did I decide to say yes to pizza this time? That's the billion-dollar question. I had driven by a little restaurant called Boston Pizza countless times and it never drew me in. In fact, when I first moved to Edmonton, I lived only two and a half blocks away from it, but I always ate at the restaurant right next door, skipping the pizza place entirely.

That night, for some reason, I said, "Sounds good, Don." And by picking pizza that night, I made one of the biggest decisions in my life, though its impact wouldn't be felt for a while. I eventually became a regular at Boston Pizza because the service was good and the food was great. I liked the look and feel of the place, and the energy. But I had no idea that soon I would learn the pizza business from Gus Agioritis, a smart guy with a black moustache and apron, and his four brothers, who also sported black moustaches and aprons. Or that I'd eventually open the first Boston Pizza franchise in BC, offering the same simple menu to brand new customers in a different market. Nor did I know that a few short years after *that* I'd partner up with a small-town accountant named George Melville, eventually buying up the entire company for $3.8 million and growing it into the billion-dollar operation that it is today, with 420 franchises in three countries. But people who think that big right out of the gate are usually a little off, or they don't make it. That night I wasn't making those kinds of big decisions—just a small one about what I was going to eat for a late-night meal.

Eighteen months after taking my first bite of pizza, more decisions followed. I eventually left the RCMP to open

Boston Pizza's first franchise, a pretty surprising decision for a guy like me. I was raised to work hard for other people, keep my head down, sock some money away, and eventually retire in a nice, comfortable community with the first gal I brought to the dance. Nothing wrong with that kind of life, except, I would soon discover, it wasn't me. In fact, it had never been for me. I just didn't know it at the time.

When did I decide to become an entrepreneur? I get asked that a lot. Total strangers come up to me when I'm out alone or with my wife, Sandi. We'll be enjoying dinner, checking into a hotel, or deplaning at an airport, and it happens. I'll make eye contact with someone. They realize they *know* me. They're *sure* they know me from somewhere. And then it clicks.

"You're that guy! You're the pizza guy! From that show! You're a Dragon, right?"

"Yes, I'm a Dragon," I'll say. (Is there a more ridiculous sentence in the English language?) I'm one of five Dragons from the hit CBC show about venture capitalism called *Dragons' Den,* one of the highest rated on TV. We're seven seasons in, but we broke through in the middle of our second season, around the time these kinds of questions started coming at me from total strangers.

Because of the show, these people, the ones who stop me in airports and restaurants, really feel like they know me. They know my businesses involve food, cars, sports, real estate and entertainment, and who doesn't like to talk about those things? *Dragons' Den* has made me a very unlikely TV star around the age when other people are thinking about retirement. And because of the show, people get to understand some of the things I'm very passionate about: partnering with talent, growing stable businesses, launching new products and fostering innovation. I also get asked if Kevin O'Leary is as mean in real life as he is on TV (no) or if Arlene Dickinson is really that kind (yes—and she's prettier in person too).

I also get questions about franchising versus opening a one-off restaurant or store. Sometimes we talk about Mr. Lube, of which my partner George Melville and I are part owners. Or we talk sports, usually hockey in particular. I'm not just a fan, I was a player and a coach, and I sit on the board of the Hockey Canada Foundation. George and I also franchise a bunch of hockey teams in the American Southwest. People who stop me often know I split my time between Dallas, Vancouver and Toronto, so I get asked about the difference between doing business across Canada and in different countries, including Mexico. So there's a lot to talk about. And when I have time, I don't mind answering those questions. But the question I get asked the most is, how did you decide to leave the daily grind of a job and become an entrepreneur?

Here's the answer: Because we ate pizza instead of Chinese that night. It's true. That very small decision, the kind of decision people make every day, turned out to be a very big decision because it changed the course of my life forever.

1

HOW I MAKE DECISIONS

"Be willing to make decisions.
That's the most important quality in a good leader."
—T. Boone Pickens

Success Is about the Big Picture

How do you know you're making the right decisions? That's another question I get asked a lot. After more than 40 years in business, I thought I would have a complicated answer. But in sitting down and writing the story of my business and my life, I've come to see that my success has been built on a series of decisions—decisions that seem to follow a pretty consistent pattern. I like simplicity. I believe that simplicity is the key to success. So my pattern seems to be this: *I make decisions about work with my heart, about money with my head, and about people with my gut.* In other words, I'm emotional about work, practical about money and instinctual about people. This method is what seems to have guided me in the right direction. But I can only say this looking back now. I certainly didn't start out in business using this method. I think it's just how I'm built. But you can train yourself to make decisions this way by watching what happens when you don't. Think about it: when you make emotional decisions about money or people, there's a lot of room for error. That's why I use my head when it comes to money. And when you make rational or emotional decisions about people, you can end up hiring the wrong person because you're biased or playing it safe. That's how a lot of companies end up with too much family on the payroll. I like to listen to my gut when it comes to hiring and partnering. It never lies to me, whereas my head and heart can. And I've never made decisions about work rationally or even instinctually; I make them with my heart. I have to love what I do. I have to feel that same passion for my work that I do for my favourite people.

Now, how do I know they're the right decisions? The outcomes. If a decision about work creates more enthusiasm, it's often the right one. If a decision about money develops more discipline, it's often the right one. And if a decision about people builds trust, it's right too.

DECISION	TOOL	OUTCOME
Work	Heart	Enthusiasm
Money	Head	Discipline
People	Gut	Loyalty/Trust

We live in a world that measures success with money, so these outcomes are not really considered popular results.

That's too bad, because the truth is, greater enthusiasm only grows businesses: it's the essence of good word of mouth. Being disciplined about money attracts investment because it quells fears in tumultuous times. And loyal partnerships and employees contribute to the longevity of a company. That's why money is a short-sighted goal. These results are always welcome because everybody benefits from them.

I've never looked at success through the lens of money. Apologies to Kevin O'Leary, my fellow Dragon, but you're wrong about this one, buddy. I learned from my dad, Ted Treliving, that success is measured by taking in the big picture: you look at the health and happiness of your family and friends and what you're contributing to your community. Success is about finding yourself and your business in a much better place than where you started out, and everyone, from employee to entrepreneur, measures that in very different ways.

So this is not a book about making more money. This is a book about making better decisions. It's about recognizing opportunities and having the ability to act on them. That's why I like to say that the harder I worked, the luckier I got.

We think good outcomes equal good decisions, bad outcomes, bad decisions. But it doesn't work like that in business or in life, really. As you'll read, many of the "worst" decisions I've ever made brought me the best outcomes possible, personally, professionally and financially. A decision is just a decision. It's neutral. It outlines an action you're going to take. It's only because of the outcome that you look back on a decision and call it good or bad.

What about the labelling of decisions as "small" or "big"? I think that's also a bit of wrong thinking. Remember, eating pizza for dinner changed the course of my life and no one would have called that a big decision. But I will say this: there *is* such a thing as easy decisions and difficult ones. Usually, the higher the stakes, the more people who are involved and the harder it is to make a decision—because you know you're setting into motion a chain of events that you may not be able to stop, events that will affect everyone and everything in their path. At the end of each chapter, I list some of the things I keep in mind when making big decisions about work, people and money.

I'm continually amazed at how *Dragons' Den* has enlivened the spirit of entrepreneurship in this country. I especially get a kick out of kids, some as young as eight years old, who can debate the merits of a business's valuation with me. I love that. And to think I almost passed on the opportunity to be a Dragon.

Here's another truth: Not everyone can get rich, but everyone can be satisfied with what they've built, with what they have, with who they are. The hallmarks of every truly successful person I know are these: they want what they have, they like what they do, and they love who they are. At the end of the day, despite the detours my decisions have taken me on, I am, I believe, exactly where I'm supposed to be, with exactly who I'm supposed to be with, doing exactly what I'm supposed to be doing. And that, to me, is the true definition of success.

2

WHO WILL I BE?

Making Your First Life Decision

"We have no simple problems or easy decisions after kindergarten."
—John W. Turk, financier

An Adult Is a Decision Maker

When you're a child, your parents make big decisions for you—hopefully good ones. As you reach adulthood, you start making your own decisions. But there's that tricky place between childhood and adulthood where your decisions can sometimes take you 10 steps forward and a few back. You're new at making them, which is why no one turns 18 without at least a few scars, inside and out. So I consider myself lucky to have come of age in a place like Virden, Manitoba. I suppose a lot of people feel the place they grew up was the most beautiful place in the world. But Virden is particularly pretty, with its fieldstone churches and Victorian buildings. Then, of course, there's the sky. Maybe that's why I took so easily to Texas, where I live today, because I love a wide-open space and a big sky. But it was a great place to grow up. I was a happy kid there, probably because I never doubted that my teachers and coaches had my best interests in mind. Because my folks were a big part of the community, shopkeepers and farmers knew me by name on Main Street. I wasn't an angel, but I never shook the idea that my behaviour would reflect on my family. So I was a pretty good kid. Though if I was going to make a bad decision, I did do my darnedest not to get caught.

Virden is a couple of hours west of Winnipeg, and like a lot of Prairie towns, it sprung up alongside the Trans-Canada rail line as it expanded across the country in the 1800s. Virden started out as a farming community, population 3,500, eventually almost doubling during the oil boom in the 1950s, when big money came to town and changed everything.

Both my grandfathers came from other countries, Scotland and England, settling in Canada in the hope of better lives. Funnily enough, when I look at my fellow panellists on *Dragons' Den,* past and present, I'm struck by the fact that almost all of them are either immigrants themselves or only one generation removed. Arlene Dickinson was born in South Africa, Robert Herjavec in Croatia, and the unforgettable Laurence Lewin in Britain. Kevin O'Leary's dad was from Ireland, his grandparents, from Lebanon, his stepdad, from Egypt. And Bruce Croxon's mother is Jamaican. While we differ in many ways, what we all have in common is the adaptability that most immigrants pass down to their kids, and a profound passion for this country. All of us are grateful, proud, enthusiastic

Canadians. And I never forget there was a slim chance I could have ended up in Australia.

The Treliving name can be traced back to the 1500s and Cornwall, England. I'm descended from a long line of naval types, so I came by my police aspirations honestly if not genetically. We ended up in Canada because of love. Before the turn of the 19th century, my British grandfather, Walter Treliving, made the wonderful mistake of falling for a pretty Irish girl named Jane Gordon. Back then, it was scandalous for an Englishman to marry an Irish woman. So he was faced with two choices: move to Canada or move to Australia. He picked Canada—Fleming, Saskatchewan, to be exact, because it was at the end of the rail line, right on the border of Manitoba, about as west as you could go at the time. (Fleming's grain elevator once graced the back of the Canadian one-dollar bill. In fact, when it burned down in 2010, it made national news.) Fleming was where my father, Ted, was born.

As a teen racking balls in a local pool hall, my dad started to apprentice with a barber who cut hair there. For the first couple of years, he worked for free. But this was at the height of the Great Depression, the dirty thirties, so good jobs were scarce in Fleming and the town didn't need two barbers. That meant the younger barber had to leave. My dad lit out on his own, nothing but a pool cue and a pair of scissors in his suitcase, and he did what a lot of young men did at the time: he moved to the closest big city. In Winnipeg, he set up his own chair at the Grain Exchange, where he made about $7 a week, a dollar of which he spent on room and board, another he kept for himself, and the rest he sent home to his family. But the big city wasn't his cup of tea. So, in the late 1930s, he took a train back to Fleming. When it made a stop in Virden, Manitoba, my dad got off. And, thinking like an entrepreneur, he soon realized the town could use a barber. He decided to stay.

Meanwhile, my grandfather on my mother's side, James Gardner, had long been settled in Virden, Manitoba. He was the entrepreneur of the family. A booming Scot, he brought his wife, Mary, to Canada from Edinburgh. He was 23 years old when he got to Virden, and it didn't take him long to find his place in the world, making friends and becoming the town's mayor, a position he held for 29 years. He was also the town's grain buyer, a central role in any farming community. So there wasn't much going on in Virden that Grandpa Gardner didn't know about or wasn't a part of. And, like I said, he was a born entrepreneur, a guy who worked for himself and made money until the day he died.

He did intend to retire. He had big plans to relax in BC after almost 30 years at the Grain Exchange. But his retirement lasted two weeks. He then bought a corner store with his son, and a few years later got involved in a gold mine. He probably would have stuck around another decade had it not been for a tragic fall from a ladder while climbing after some peaches. His broken hip got infected and he died at the age of 93. He was a great man, and as much as I inherited a military bent from my paternal grandfather, Walter Treliving, I like to think I got my entrepreneurial spirit from Grandpa Gardner.

In Virden, my dad at first dated my mother's sister, Rita, but after a few weeks, he decided she was not for him. Then he became smitten with Rita's quieter sister, Mina. Mina and Ted married in 1940, when my dad was 37 years old; my mother had just finished high school. I was born a year later. It was considered a pretty big age difference between my folks—then and now. But my father had deliberately waited that long to marry. He didn't want to get married until he had saved enough money to actually afford a family. And by "afford" I mean he waited until he had enough money to pay for a house—cash, no mortgage—and to ensure that his wife would never have to work outside the home. On a barber's income, that took a while. There was none of this "We'll build something together" or "We can survive on love." My dad felt that a solid financial foundation was as important as love when it came to marriage, if not more so. And there was no borrowing from the bank. He was of the mind that a man provided and until he could provide he was not a man.

We lived near the training base for Commonwealth pilots, and my earliest memory is of planes flying overhead, during World War II. I have a picture of me in my dad's arms, pointing at the sky. Then we moved to a beautiful two-storey Victorian a block from downtown, originally built by a doctor who died before his family could move in. My father paid cash for that house, about $1,500. He bought nothing on credit, unless you counted my mother's shopping. In those days, you could do all your shopping on the honour system. My mother would buy something at the clothing store and the clerk would write down her purchase. She'd do the same thing at Bill Baird's butcher shop, then make a stop for other groceries at Scales and Rothnie. And every Monday morning my dad did the rounds, paying each store on his way to work. After my younger sister, Joy, and I were old enough to fend for ourselves, my mother actually got a job at the grocery store, which lasted all of a couple of hours. When my dad came home from work that day, my mother announced that, come Monday, she too had a job to go to. My dad wasn't amused. He made her go back to the grocer's and quit. No wife of his was going to work, he said. Shortly after that, she became pregnant with a late-in-life baby, my sister Pat, who became the apple of my dad's eye. What can I say? My parents were a product of their times. And if my mother ever resented my father, she never showed it. She was devoted to him.

In high school, I had two very different sets of friends. Playing sports meant I hung out with the jocks, but I also hung out with the so-called bad kids—the future criminals, according to my dad. I've always found myself at ease in various worlds. This skill paid off later as a police officer and, of course, as a restaurant owner.

The other thing about Virden was that it had no class system—everyone seemed to have the same things, make the same amount of money, have the same worries and joys. Or so I thought. Money—who had it, who didn't—wasn't something I thought much about until the Turnbull boys came over to our house one winter morning for a visit. Bad enough they were only wearing rubber boots in the snow, but when my mother saw that they didn't have any socks on, her face went white with concern.

"Boys, where are your socks?" she asked, trying to not sound too alarmed.

They shyly replied that they didn't have any.

"Oh well, lucky for you, Jim's got lots of socks," she said, running upstairs to grab them a handful to take home. She did this quickly and cheerfully, so as not to make a fuss and embarrass my friends. The things I took for granted!

We might have had more than others, but we were far from rich. In fact, we didn't own a car until my dad could afford to buy one outright. Even then, my mother did all the driving. My father was a sharp, cautious man, but a disaster behind the wheel.

Our first car was a 1954, two-toned Chevy Bel Air. My dad wouldn't buy a Lincoln, the car wealthier folks in town drove. He didn't want to alienate his customers, who would be turned off if they saw their barber driving a fancier car than theirs. He understood such social subtleties. Fancy cars were beginning to appear on Main Street at an alarming rate—a new model every day—driven by total strangers who were beginning to populate the town. We eyed them suspiciously because we knew something was up. I can't say exactly when our small town became a medium-sized town or when the focus turned from farming to oil, but somewhere in the mid-1950s, things really began to change.

Money Changes People . . . and Places

There had been rumours that people drilling for water wells in and around Virden were hitting natural gas veins. That meant one thing: oil wasn't too far below. The McIvors were the first to hit oil, in 1954. Shortly after that, a geological team came in to do some seismic work, and sure enough, it found a big oil field about 1,750 feet down, just a mile outside Virden.

An entirely new thing arrived in town: not just oil, but money—and all the industries that go along with making it. It's incredible to witness a sleepy town wake up, change and go in a different direction. All of a sudden there was a huge influx of people coming from all over North America: BC, Alberta, the Maritimes, even Oklahoma and Texas, their kids with their funny accents filling our classrooms. Streets were lined with big trucks. Butler steel sheds popped up everywhere to house equipment. My dad usually worked until 10 p.m. cutting hair. I was a teenager, so to me it was all exciting—it felt like things were finally happening in Virden. My dad, however, remained cautious, quietly eyeing the changes from his barbershop in the centre of town.

Before the boom, my dad had bought the building that housed his shop, leasing part of it to a bank. At the back of the building was a room he rented to an oil survey company—which meant that if a farm was being scoped out, my dad was often one of the first to know about it. I worked as a rod man for a while, helping the survey teams working in the field. In 1955 alone, over 350 oil wells were drilled in and around Virden. That's also around the time my dad earned the nickname "The Banker," his barbershop being the first stop farmers would make after an oil company offered to drill on their land. They knew my dad dealt in cash because that's how he was paid and tipped. Farming, on the other hand, wasn't a cash business. Loans from banks were paid off after the sale of the previous year's crops. Advances to finance the next year's crops were based on the success of the current yield. The idea that under those crops could be a more lucrative way to make a buck—well, you can imagine why farmers clamoured after those oil company contracts. But securing oil rights often involved a lot of paperwork. Paperwork meant lawyers and accountants, and they cost money. Farmers would borrow that money from my father interest-free, sometimes offering him small percentages of those rights, which was the roundabout way my dad got into the oil business. A lot of those transactions were done on a handshake. One farmer, Elmer McLean, who was a good friend of my dad's, struck oil on his farm and persuaded Dad to buy a small percentage of his rights. There was never a formal contract, just a handshake, but to this day my family receives residual cheques from that well.

The boom was good for the local economy but not necessarily good for vulnerable families. My dad watched as people mortgaged their lives to hit oil. A close friend of his tried to convince him to invest heavily in the speculation business. But my dad just wasn't interested. His friend, however, put everything on the line. Luckily for him, he did strike it rich. But he also got a stern lecture from my dad about risking his family's security on a business venture. That's still quite a big trigger for me. When I hear pitches on *Dragons' Den* from entrepreneurs boasting about the lengths to which they'd gone to back a venture, lengths that include putting their home on the line or cashing in their retirement savings or children's education funds, I feel angry. I'm all for risks you can afford. And entrepreneurship is about nothing if not taking risks. But if it means cashing in your family's financial security, you probably can't afford to take that risk. It's that simple.

Even though my dad was getting plenty of offers and there was plenty of opportunity, he just didn't feel that tug towards the oil business. Instead of seeing an easier life with less work and more money, my dad saw the dark side: problem drinkers becoming alcoholics and shaky marriages falling completely apart at the first sign of wealth. Now that couples could afford to split up, they did, rather than try to work things out. Kids were indulged and went wild. Parents bought their teenagers brand new cars that ended up in the junk pile after a few flips. My dad's theory was that because these kids hadn't saved up to buy their own cars, they didn't have the incentive to take better care of them, to be more cautious. So what if they crash? Their parents would just buy them another one. And they often did, with tragic results. One day I drove out to a bowling alley in Brandon with a bunch of friends. After a few rounds, we again split up between the two vehicles to head back to Virden. Five of my friends left just after me. All five were killed on the highway back to town. Fast money brought a certain sense of abandon, and even I almost got caught up in it, forgoing my dream of becoming a police officer to chase easy money.

Since I was a boy I had wanted to wear the Red Serge of the Royal Canadian Mounted Police. The Mounties had a mythic quality on the Prairies. We learned in school that they were initially a frontier force, policing the wilds of northern Canada and keeping the peace during the Yukon gold rush. I wanted in. But before I even turned 18, I had started to turn a buck on the rigs, making more money than any new recruit could ever make. That was a dangerous place to linger, between a dream and a paycheque. Money is a very powerful draw, and for boys like me in Virden, it often won out over school or other aspirations.

Teachers Aren't Always Right

I've always loved hard work, and I love earning money. My first job was delivering newspapers for $2 a week. Then I delivered groceries in an old hearse for $6 a week (for the Adams family, if you can believe it). When the boom hit, I lied about my age. You had to be 18 to work the rigs. I was 16, but I was big, so I easily scored a job making $2.10 an hour, a small fortune—more than my dad made cutting hair.

All of a sudden I had cash. My friends had cash too. We bought a lot more of everything that was available. We bought cars, we spoiled our dates, we took trips. University enrolment suffered a big drop-off. Why would you want to go to school for four years when there was fast money to be made? And I didn't need any excuse to skip out on school. Trust me, I always fought school hard. Every report card ever issued to me said the same thing: *Jim has all the ability in the world, but he doesn't apply himself. Jim never pays attention. He's always socializing with the other students.* One teacher suggested I get a job in forestry. It's the only thing she said I was good for: outdoor manual labour, in a remote area, far from trouble. I'll be forever grateful to my parents, who never let me be discouraged by that kind of criticism. They didn't blindly encourage me either. Instead, they nudged me in the direction where I'd shine, where I'd be good at something. They helped me be the best version of *me* that I could be. True, I was no scholar, but I never doubted I'd be successful, that there was a place for me in the world and that if I applied myself I'd find it.

I worked as a roughneck, outside on the rig's deck connecting 16-foot lengths of pipes that stretched down 1,700 feet and more. Once we hit oil, my job was to pull that pipe back up, send acid down to burn through the sandstone, then push the pipe back down until it poked through the softened rock to oil. It was the kind of work that went from tedious to dangerous with pretty much nothing in the middle. One day a guy on my shift lost an arm at the elbow because he wasn't paying attention. We received no specialized training, just a few hours of muttering and pointing by some older guy who'd worked there a little longer than we had. Back then there was no workers' compensation if you got injured. It was just very hard work, stretched over very long hours in faraway places where you lived for days and weeks with little to no time off. But it was very, very lucrative. So this was the first big decision I faced: Stick to the rigs and make a buck, or become an RCMP officer and wear the Red Serge?

Money Creates Momentum, Not Enthusiasm

At the beginning of every successful venture I've been a part of, I'm seized by a wave of emotion, a tug, a feeling of enthusiasm. My imagination is lit up. My heart pumps faster when I think about it. When I thought about becoming an RCMP officer, that's how I felt. So I had never struggled with that decision—that is, until I started to make a lot of money working the rigs. Then, for the first time in my life, I began to question a decision I had made. The money was that good. In fact, working the rigs I could make twice, even three times what a police officer made, more if I got lucky with speculations. So if I was going to stay on the rigs, I had to get my mind around more than just a good paycheque. I knew I would have to feel enthusiastic about the whole damn thing, not just the money. I'd have to love the actual physical job, the people, the environment, and the routine, daily grind of it all. I had to feel enthusiastic about the work first or the job would be dead in the water.

I'm the type of guy that, if I don't love what I'm doing, I can't do it for very long. And that's the first step towards building anything of value. You know that old saying, do what you love and the money will follow? Making a lot of money and building anything of value takes time. You can't achieve that in a job you don't like, because you'll continually interrupt your own progress. It's that simple.

I knew right away I would hate a life on the rigs. So that first big decision was easy. I chose to pursue what I loved to do over the money I loved to make. Why? Because when I thought about becoming a police officer, I felt enthused. I began to imagine a life where every day I faced a different dilemma or adventure, where I moved around the country, helping people solve problems, keeping the country safe. I've always been attracted to the combination of discipline and unpredictability that police work is all about. I think it's in my genes. I was part of the militaristic Treliving clan, so becoming an RCMP officer was an easy fit. On the other side, I had the entrepreneurial Gardner blood, which embraced unpredictability.

Here's another thing about using enthusiasm to help you make decisions about work: it's not something you can lie about. You can't fake enthusiasm. I could imagine being deeply satisfied by the actual work of being a police officer. And that was very true for me, until a different kind of work fired up my imagination. But the decision that led to that was still a few years away.

There was a small part of me that worried. What if I don't like it? What if I'm no good at being an RCMP officer? I was too young, really, to know there would be options, that there would *always* be options. But the thing about making work decisions informed by enthusiasm is that it doesn't really matter what happens after you make the decision—you're already well on your way to success.

Now, you might be scratching your head at that idea. But bear with me. Here's how I think it works: enthusiasm will always provide the momentum needed to get traction in your chosen field, even if you have to eventually make a detour. If I choose work I love, you'd have to knock me on the head and drag me home in a sack to get me to take a break. That's how I'm wired. And that's why enthusiasm is my goal when it comes to deciding the right work path. And enthusiasm comes from the heart.

However, here's what I think would have happened had I decided to work on the rigs for big money. My first few months would have been great. I would have made a lot of money, and because I would have still been living at home, I'd have cultivated a skewed sense of life's true cost. Then there would have been a blur of buying: a nice car, a new set of clothes, some fancy dates and trips. Great stuff. And trust me, I'd have enjoyed every living minute of it—especially considering the reality of a police officer's salary (which for me meant a damp basement apartment, a stream of roommates, crappy takeout and no dating because I couldn't afford it). But after the shiny paycheque loses its lustre, then what? A kind of depression would have kicked in. There is no darker place for me than when I'm slogging away at work that doesn't fuel my spirit. There is no greater way to make me feel worse about myself, and about life in general. Success doesn't gravitate to people who give off negativity. And no paycheque can pull you out of that kind of slump. In fact, really, those big cheques create only one thing: debt. Then you're married to work you don't like in order to pay off debt you've accumulated to try to stave off your depression. People lose decades in brutal financial cycles of this sort—making good money, creating big debt, and then slogging away to pay it off.

I was all of 19 when I left the rigs behind and headed to RCMP training in Regina. The timing was perfect: I was getting into a little bit of trouble with my "bad boy" crowd. At one point I was dating one of my teachers *and* the town's hairdresser. One night, I found myself sneaking out the back door of the salon as the teacher was coming through the front door for a haircut. While I was pulling on my shoes in the alley, a friend of my dad's walked by. Soon after, my dad sat me down for The Talk. The party was over, he said. Time to leave home and embark on my adult life. It was time for me to start making bigger decisions on my own.

My dad would have liked me to be more scholarly, to have gone to university. He had only a grade eight education himself, but he read *Life* and *National Geographic* magazines religiously. He saw the world through those articles and pictures, and he had always imagined a bigger life for me, bigger than being a young dad and husband. Nothing wrong with that, but he knew I was the restless type. So a few months after sneaking out of that hair salon as a bratty teenage boy on the make, I found myself in Regina holding the reins of a moody horse, and wearing brown fatigues and a forge cap with a yellow band. You didn't get fitted for the iconic Red Serge until you graduated. And let me tell you, although I was young and scared, I was very happy. *So even if a decision feels "off," and on the surface things aren't very settled, if there's still a deep sense of contentedness, I know I've made the right decision.*

Stress Breaks or Bonds People

All RCMP recruits did their training in Regina. First came the written exams: a bit of math, some science, and a 1,500-word essay on why you wanted to be an RCMP officer. Only 500 men were accepted out of the thousands of applicants from across the country. At six foot four, I almost didn't make the cut. To ride the horses, you couldn't be taller than six foot six; I slid in by two inches. The first thing I realized in basic training was that the horses were treated better than the recruits. Training took about a year, and it was the toughest thing I've ever endured.

We slept 32 to a room on cots covered with a fitted sheet, a straight sheet, a blanket and a pillow. Sometimes we slept on top of the blankets because it was faster that way to get ready in the morning. (Instructors took great pleasure in coming behind you and messing up a carefully made bed, which would cause you to be penalized.) When we weren't cleaning the stables or fending off senior recruits who stole our lunches, we'd be marching . . . and marching some more, the whole time listening to instructors telling us to go home to "mommy," whispering we weren't police material, that we were "babies," not man enough to be Mounties. This was designed to break anyone who was beginning to have doubts. Here's the rationale: If you can't stand a bit of abuse, you're going to crack in the field, where police offi-cers are routinely taunted and disrespected when trying to do their jobs. So we had to toughen up fast.

Physical training was another kind of torture altogether. We did calisthenics in rooms with the heat turned up so high that some guys vomited or fainted. Rifle training, pis-tol training, combat training, boxing—all were relentless exercises that left recruits bruised and bloodied.

One of the most interesting parts of my RCMP training was learning how to read people using our instincts. They'd throw up these overhead photographs and film clips of sus-pects, witnesses and convicted criminals. We wouldn't be given their names or the natures of the crimes right away. But we were taught to read facial expressions, to look at their eyes and study what they focused on, to watch how they sat, behaved, spoke and moved. If the criminals looked up, down, right or left during an interrogation, that told us something about them, usually that they were lying, fright-ened, hiding something or being evasive. We'd study the way sweat beaded on the face and the way tension worked its way around the mouth and eyes and what that meant—to us. Beyond what their behaviour told us about them, we were learning how to hone our natural abilities to read people.

We are rarely wrong about people. If we think some-one's lying or dangerous, they probably are. But we're conditioned to be polite. We're taught not to hurt people's feelings. So we override our instincts and end up putting ourselves in bad situations with bad people. Learning to be a good cop is to get back in touch with the gut feeling that's telling you the truth about someone. It's remained an invaluable skill for me, and it's become the cornerstone of my decision-making process in both business and life.

Eventually, we dug into the Criminal Code, read case studies, did some role-playing and studied psychological profiling. We didn't delve too far into provincial statutes, as we didn't know yet which province we'd be sent to at the end of training.

Yes, it was hard, and yes, many times I wanted to quit. But I'll tell you why I stuck it out: my F-Troop mates, my fellow Mounties-in-training. When we lost heart, we'd draw on each other's strength and stamina. Notice the use of the word "we" in my recounting of the experience. We trained, we ate, we marched, we fought, we studied, we learned, we respected one another. There is a certain bonding that happens within a group of people when you go through something stressful collectively. You're in it together. RCMP training is supposed to be tough. It's supposed to scare you. It's supposed to make you question your decision to become a police officer. That's how those who aren't that serious or are too weak for the task are weeded out. But throughout the training we were reminded again and again of one simple fact: If one member of our troop strays or disappoints, the whole troop gets walloped.

Mounties were bred like that back then, to be a tight team, to rely on each other, to have each other's backs. We put group principles first, our individual needs and personalities second. To this day, more than 50 years later, I still receive near daily emails from some of my former troop mates. A while ago, I loaded a bunch of them onto a private jet in Vancouver, to visit another troop mate in Calgary. I've watched their kids grow up. Some have been through divorces and illnesses. We're tight for life because we'd been through trying times and made it through training only because of our collective strength, our esprit de corps.

At the end, we graduated with the best of the best. Ours was an 11-month course. Today, training time is half that—about 24 weeks. I don't believe that's enough time to form the crucial bond between people that builds loyalty. I frequently hear from retired RCMP officers who say the biggest problem with the police force these days is the length of training. They say it's too short, the standards have grown lax, that it's too easy to become a member. I'll reserve my opinion about that, as I haven't been a police officer for a few decades, but drawing from my entrepreneurial experience, if developing enthusiasm is a given at the start of a new adventure, then good solid training is the single most important element in maintaining it.

Enthusiasm is a muscle. You don't go to the gym for a month, get fit, and never go back. You have to develop a program to constantly strengthen and maintain your muscles. To stay enthusiastic you have to find a way to tap back into the original desire that led you on that path to begin with. That's why I caution people who look to my life and think that it's the money that gives me satisfaction and determines my success. It's not the money. It's the work. Period. It's always been about love of the work and the resulting enthusiasm. That's why I always make work decisions with my heart, not my head, and not even my gut.

Indecision Is the Death of Options

It was a snowy February day when I arrived in Prince George, BC, the backseat of my blue, 1960 Chevy Bel Air stuffed with clothes, including my RCMP uniforms. I pulled into the Phillips 66 gas station on First Avenue to get directions to the local dispatch for my first day of my first posting, changing into my Red Serge in the washroom at the Simon Fraser Hotel across the street. Then I went over to introduce myself at my new detachment. I felt complete. That's the only word I can use to describe what it felt like to finally wear that iconic uniform. In fact, I think my enthusiasm for the job entered the building before I did.

At the desk, I stopped, saluted and said, "J.W. Treliving reporting for duty."

The corporal on duty looked me up and down slowly, then said, "Holy shit, get a load of the shine on this one."

Other guys scattered around the office laughed. I must have looked so earnest, so ready, so keen, but inside I felt suddenly deflated. I drove halfway across the country, only to be greeted like this? If I was upset, I never let them see it. Not a time to show any weakness.

"Do you have a place to stay?"

"No, sir."

"No, *corporal*. You address me as 'corporal.' You know better than that."

"Yes, corporal."

He directed me to the Travelodge around the corner that sometimes rented rooms long term.

"See if you can rent a room for a month. That's about how long you'll last here. And another thing, Treliving: Go change out of that uniform before you get shot. You're a big, fat red target."

I stayed at the Travelodge for a couple of months before renting a basement apartment with a few other guys. What can I say about Prince George? Back then it was a hell of a tough town, a place where people were either drinking and fighting or sleeping it off. Locals carried concealed weapons. Knifings and robberies were common crimes. A favourite spectator sport was hauling up a lawn chair in front of the Canada Hotel to watch Mounties break up fights. It was UFC before there was UFC. Well-paying jobs in mining and forestry were the big draws of the town. So it was a transient population that included a lot of Eastern bloc immigrants who'd come to Canada after some revolution or another, often trailing criminal records. They were the types who worked hard, played hard and fought harder still.

The downside of working in Prince George was that I opened a lot of files, more than my fellow police officers who were sent to tamer places like Saskatoon or Edmonton. The upside of working in Prince George was that I opened a lot of files. Every case was different. And every time the phone rang, I got another swift lesson in western justice. This was trial by fire, being thrown right into a fast-growing town, much like the ones that sprouted up during the gold rush days—the kind of places that made even good citizens make bad decisions. But it was ultimately in Prince George that I honed one of the most important skills a police officer possesses: making decisions and then acting on them quickly.

Bad Decisions Are Rooted in Fear

On one of my first patrols, we were alerted that a robbery was in progress at a warehouse on the outskirts of town. I was green as all get-out, but we were trained in how to enter a building, armed and alert to potential trouble. We spent hours and hours going through drills, doing what you see police do in countless TV shows, rounding corners with guns at the ready, whispering and gesturing to each other to get into the ideal position to pounce. What those shows can't ever really show is the adrenaline that courses through your veins when you know something's up behind closed doors, yet you don't know exactly what awaits you. That feeling can either urge you on or completely paralyze you. I've seen it. I've felt it. It's as though there's a wall of fear you have to push through.

Arriving at the warehouse that night, we entered the building quietly. We flicked the light switch but remained in the pitch-black. The suspects had taken out the lights. You couldn't see your fingers in front of your face. But you could hear people moving around. The suspects had an advantage. They were already in position and accustomed to the dark. This was bad. Everything in me wanted to leave, but my training kept me grounded, and propelled me a step forward. We were taught never to freeze, always to push through fear. Take action. Any action, so long as you take it and keep moving. You can't think. You can't second-guess yourself. You can't overanalyze. You make a decision, and then you act. We kept creeping forward into the dark, urging whoever was in the building to yield. Moments later, I sensed something near me. I stuck out my hand and felt hair, then grabbed someone by the collar. My partner snagged another man near him. They had frozen in fear, becoming easy targets. We pushed through it and caught them.

Another time, while patrolling the streets with a fellow police officer, we heard gunshots coming from the local jewellers'. (Gunshots are never as deep and booming as they sound on TV cop shows and westerns; they sound more like curbside firecrackers.) We cautiously approached the front door of the store. We could see that just inside the shop a suspect lay moaning in a puddle of his own blood. Seemed the owner of the store, who'd been robbed before, shot the intruder and was now holed up in a panic behind the counter, unwilling to surrender. I assured him that we were RCMP officers only trying to help. He didn't believe us. He couldn't be reasoned with. My partner suggested I throw my hat into the store to prove we were police officers.

"Good idea." I gently tossed in my felt hat. Just before it landed on the ground, the storeowner shot a hole clean through the middle of it. For a 77-year-old jeweller, he had pretty darn good aim.

But one of the most memorable lessons I took with me

from my time as a police officer is that everyone has a value system—everyone, even criminals, has a set of principles they live by. They're just buried under layers of bad deeds and guilty consciences. In fact, the best of them, the most organized and successful criminals I've known, live by a code of ethics as sacred as any I've come across among law-abiding citizens. I also realized that it's usually fear, not bad character, that causes people to make stupid decisions.

I remember a case where a storeowner was robbed and killed, her throat slit from ear to ear. It was a real tragedy, the kind of thing that leaves a town shaken and wary. Thanks to rumours and instinct, we picked up a suspect, someone well known to us for this kind of crime and this kind of weapon. But we couldn't find enough evidence to support the case. There were no witnesses. My partner and I were furious, certain that we had the right guy. But ultimately, we didn't have the proof to nail him. Before he left the detachment, I had a quiet word with him.

"We didn't get you this time," I said. "But we will. And know this: For the rest of your life, no matter where you go, or where you live, or how far away from this deed you think you are, know you're being watched. Know that every police officer in every corner of this country, and this world, will follow you, and they'll know about you, because I'm going to spend the rest of my life making sure of that. We have our eye on you. You step out of line—and you will step out of line—they'll bring you back. To me."

Young police officers are nothing if not passionate. So I'm not excusing what I said. But let's say, for argument's sake, that I was wrong about him. Let's say this fellow wasn't the murderer. Fine. If that were the case, then my words might have slid right off his clear conscience, and I would have been just a jerky police officer making some macho, idle threats.

Instead, here's what happened. Months later, he moved to Port Coquitlam to get away from all the eyes on him in Prince George—because we were, in fact, keeping an eye on him. So he left town, and moved . . . right next door to a highway patrolman. Every night the unsuspecting RCMP officer parked his squad car in the driveway, and every night this guy peeked from behind the curtains next door, more and more convinced that we had found him and were coming to get him. A few months later he turned himself in to the local detachment, his nerves completely shot. He said he had to confess to a murder he committed in Prince George because he knew that the officer next door was there to eventually pick him up. I love this story because it suggests that, deep down inside, each of us has a moral core. After all, who really *was* watching this guy? No one but himself.

But it was another incident that highlighted one of the principles I was most lacking in, which, if I didn't cultivate it, would get me into a lot of trouble. And that was discipline. Without discipline, your decisions have no muscle, no consistency.

Decisions without Discipline Are Weak

On the outskirts of Prince George, a man drove by what he thought was a large animal dying at the side of the road.

He stopped in at the RCMP office where I was stationed at the time and suggested we check it out. My partner and I got into my car and drove to the spot he described. As we pulled over, we realized it wasn't a dog or a deer but a naked woman, beaten from head to toe and covered in an inch of road dust. She was still alive. After we got her to the hospital and found out who she was and where she lived, I drove to her house alone to question her husband, who was known for putting bruises on her before. This time, she said, he'd used a horse harness.

He met me on the gravel driveway, drunk and defiant. I was alone, blinded by anger and youth. It occurred to me that, despite the evidence, he could still get away with it. He had so far. At the first sign of provocation, I lunged at him and put him in a headlock. As I held him firmly, it did cross my mind how easy it would be to make that headlock fatal. I was trained to do this, after all—to hold a person until they passed out. I also knew how to snap a neck like a chicken's if things got out of hand or I was threatened. And who would miss this guy? Would the world be a lesser place without him? I have to admit, these were my thoughts.

Seconds later, my troop mate pulled up the driveway. He saw me holding the guy in a tight grip. He approached me with the same caution you'd use to close in on an agitated suspect. He knew what I was thinking of doing before he even got out of the car.

"Jim," he said gently, his hand up. "Don't. It's not worth it. He's not worth it."

I released the guy, and he fell to the floor coughing.

The woman pulled through, though barely. She was blind and walked with a limp for the rest of her life.

I am still ashamed to say that during the man's trial, I gave the worst testimony of my life. It was full of bias, opinion, anger and bluster. I was not objective. This was not good police work.

"Of all the people I've picked up, this guy's the worst," I said angrily, my emotions getting the better of me.

When the judge gave the man a mere two years less a day, with the option of parole, I huffed, and loudly. The judge hit his gavel on the block.

"I heard that, Constable Treliving!" he said. "You are not the juror or the judge. That is my job. The best you can do is take him off the street. You did that. Enough out of you."

On the stand that day, I forgot I was a police officer. I forgot my job was to serve and protect, to apprehend suspects and let the rest of the justice system take over. Instead, I was an angry man who wanted to take revenge on a known violent offender because the person he beat wasn't able to. I wanted justice for her. But what if my testimony had caused a mistrial? Then where would justice be?

I think I was a good police officer for the most part. But, as I said, discipline was a challenge for me, and I wore my emotions on my sleeve. It took a lot of training to cultivate my "ice face," the stern, flat look you see some police officers wear so that they remain unreadable and seemingly unmoved in tense situations. You can't show vulnerability. Even in business, it's never a good idea for your competitors to know you're worried or afraid. But discipline's a skill. Luckily, both as a police officer and as an entrepreneur, I have always been partnered with people who are more disciplined than I am.

My first year as an RCMP officer, I made about $50 every two weeks working 14 days straight, with no day off. A year and a half later, I was making $400 a month. Not bad, but my roommates and I still mostly threw house parties instead of going out on the town, and we stayed close together. We saved money that way, but we also avoided hanging out with the general population. It wasn't a good idea in a place like Prince George to hang out with the locals. The police weren't considered allies of the people, there to guard and protect, so much as they were considered nuisances to the local criminals who menaced the streets of that city. It was a tough realization to come to. To me, growing up, police officers were heroes. In Prince George, not so much.

I was, eventually, transferred to Edmonton, and I thought I'd never see Prince George again. I was wrong. In just a few years I'd return, but this time wearing a very different uniform.

Checklist for Making
the First Life Decision

This is one of the first big decisions we make after high school: to go to university or not. To get a job or kick-start a career. And most of us are still teenagers when we're asked to do this, still living at home, still wet behind the ears—or at least I sure was. So here are some essential things to keep in mind when making that first big decision:

1. Don't Look to the Money. So many times I'm approached by someone—a friend, a stranger, it doesn't matter—who wants to start a new business and hopes to run the idea by me. If I have time, I say, shoot. Nine times out of 10, they'll start the story with the numbers. They tell me how much money this product or business is going to make. They talk about the margins, the profits and the growth potential. My first question is always, "Why do you want to do this kind of work?" And I wait for the pause. They think for a second, then scratch their heads. "What do you mean, why?" they'll say. "I'm talking about making a lot of money!" But I want to know, do you like the work? Are you enthusiastic about the idea of going to the office or the shop floor every day? Does what you're manufacturing or doing make your heart race? Can you imagine yourself working at this all day, every day? You should feel a bit consumed by it; it should occupy your thoughts the way meeting a new guy or gal does. So I want to know if they feel that certain tug at the heart towards the work or the idea. If this question baffles them, I'm fairly certain they're in for a world of pain.

Money's a great thing, but it makes you want things, some of which you can afford, some of which you can't. Before skipping school for a great-paying job, know there will come a day when good money's not going to be enough to get your butt out of bed in the morning. If you still want to go that route, make sure you put other things in place that'll get your juices flowing when your work doesn't. Which leads me to . . .

2. Pursue Your Passions. If there are people who've become successful doing something they hate, I don't know them. By "successful" I mean that overall sense of well-being that includes a skip to the step and a lust for life. This is why I make work decisions with my heart, not my head or my gut. If I had done that, I would have stayed on the rigs where my head told me I'd make a lot of money fast, and my gut told me I'd be good at it. I had my heart set on being a Mountie, and I'll be forever grateful for that decision. It led me everywhere after.

3. Always Look to the Work. If you're young and reading this for some guidance in making this first big decision, or if you're wondering which direction to take in your professional life, here's one piece of advice: Start with imagining yourself in your work environment—the office, the cubicle, the factory floor, the cab of the truck, the kitchen, the studio floor. Get into the nitty-gritty details. Will you drive, walk, or take transit to this work? Picture the commute. Picture yourself there, day and night, doing the "do" of that particular job. Is there a window near you? Who's around you? If you feel that tug, that sense of enthusiasm, filling you from the shoes up, you'll know you've found a place you can start to plant the seeds of your dream. It's the beginning of your journey.

Ignore the bottom line; tune out the folks who try to sell you on the lucrative side of the business or idea. Get down to the gut level about the actual daily work involved. Can you picture doing it, enjoying it, and most important, showing other people how to do it too? It's a key step that's often missed. The story of your work is how you recruit like-minded people to climb aboard and join you in your vision, whether as employees, partners or investors. If there is no enthusiasm for the work, you'll sense it at the gut level, and so will other people. Prospective clients, potential employees or partners will read your ambivalence, your fear, your boredom and they will not join you. At least, the right people won't. And you won't be able to pass on your knowledge to the next generation of employees, partners or investors. Your business will die on the vine.

I can't stress this enough. Picture what you'll be actually doing at work, not what you'll do with the money you earn. Lots of people get this backwards and pick careers based on outcomes: actors seeking fame instead of perfecting a craft, autoworkers looking only for benefits, teachers who want their summers off instead of a career inspiring the next generation of kids. That way of thinking is a recipe for misery.

4. Strife Builds Strength. Despite my enthusiasm for my chosen field, I almost quit during RCMP training—it was that tough. But I came from a family where there was no drama, no strife, no fighting, no problems that couldn't be solved. We were, to put it simply, the Cleavers of the Prairies. So, at 18, I was pushed out into the world a little soft in the head, hands and heart, the very tools I employ now to make decisions. I had no edge to me, no idea what the real world was about and what kind of dramas were in store for me. Nothing truly bad had ever happened to me. I wanted to be a police officer because the job played to the strengths I knew I did have. I was a big, imposing guy, so I had presence. I was athletic, so I had strength. I liked the feeling of doing the right thing, even if I didn't always do it myself. And frankly, I respected my country and its laws. My values lined up with the values of the institution.

Those are all pretty good reasons to become a police officer. Add to those things the excitement factor—the horses, the fast cars, becoming skilful with weapons—and you had the makings of a keen recruit. But I didn't have discipline, and I had never committed to anything really tough. During our training, I built up my stamina. I learned how to persevere. And I did it by bonding with a bunch of guys who were going through the same hell I was, guys who are still my friends today because of it. I developed that crucial stick-to-it-iveness I'd eventually need as an entrepreneur.

5. Enthusiasm Creates Wealth. Trust this statement, because it's the truth.

Enthusiasm also creates stamina. When you can work like a dog with joy in your heart, you're going to make more money. If you're trudging along, as I did on the rigs, you'll sabotage that financial flow because you won't attract the right people to your cause. Or you'll get frozen out of opportunities because of your attitude, or worse, fired. People like to make these matters complicated, but they're really that simple. Enthusiastic people attract the same. As a group, enthusiasts create momentum, and money loves momentum. Passionate people doing something they love will always attract the right people to them. I think if George and I are known for anything in our organization, it's the unbridled enthusiasm for what we do and what we have. We didn't grow a successful company with just the two of us. We grew it with the dozens of talented executives we were lucky to team up with and the hundreds more talented franchisees who spread the vision of our company. We grew wealth by spreading our enthusiasm and generating even more. It's that simple.

3

DO I WANT A JOB, OR DO I WANT TO CREATE JOBS?

On Becoming a Decision Maker

"The harder I work, the luckier I get."
—Samuel Goldwyn, movie producer

Creatures of Habit Miss Opportunity

Edmonton wasn't nearly as haywire as Prince George but it was still a western city, full of bravado and beer, if a little more cosmopolitan. There was also a much heartier ethnic population opening restaurants and running businesses. And there was oil money in Edmonton, which meant people could buy things that others wanted to steal. So police officers were busy. And though change can be unnerving to some, I am definitely enlivened by change; I love it. But here's the thing: I also love familiarity. So as much as I was excited about being transferred to another city, one I'd never been to before, I also loved that the RCMP had the same rules, same uniforms, and same protocols in Edmonton as it did in Prince George, and indeed, across Canada. Funny enough, balancing those two opposing forces, newness and familiarity, is at the very core of building and operating a successful franchise. More on franchise building later, but that skill was first honed in the RCMP, which in a way is itself a successful franchise.

The first thing I noticed about Alberta was that there was more respect for RCMP officers than in northern BC. You felt that right away. They loved us in Edmonton. We always got a salute and a nod. So this was a welcome change, and it was nice to feel gratitude. For me, it was a much-needed boost. I was still pretty enthusiastic about police work, but not so much about paperwork, and it seemed to me that the bigger the city, the more forms we had to fill out. My rough-and-tumble career of ducking under yellow police lines and sipping coffee on a stakeout in the early hours of the morning was beginning to involve a lot more yellow pencils being pushed around a big wooden desk. Something a little like boredom had begun to creep in.

I was newly married to a nurse named Elaine Tkatchuk, who I had met at a dance in Regina. She was a Ukrainian farm girl who was just finishing nursing school. After she graduated, I drove from Prince George to marry her on her family's farm in Saskatchewan. She briefly joined me in Prince George. Then she came out with me to Edmonton.

We first moved to The Alhambra, two and a half blocks from a little place called Boston Pizza. I walked by it a lot, but never went in. The apartment was pricey, costing $85 a month, and for the year and a half that we lived there, Elaine and I rarely ate out. When we did have money, we chose Chinese food because it was cheaper and I knew my way around the menu. Truthfully, I didn't really know what pizza was or how to eat it. And the sign didn't say "Boston Restaurant" or "Boston Italian." It said "Boston Pizza." And if you weren't familiar with the dish, why would you go? As I said, I love familiarity, so I could be a real creature of habit. Police officers are like that. You have your spots, your favourite places, where they know you and you know them. We like routine.

I had an uncle who was an Edmonton city police officer, and he soon introduced me to a colleague of his, Don Spence. Don was around my age and single at the time. He was a stocky guy, very personable, always up for a party. We became fast friends, getting together after our shifts to grab a bite to eat and unwind. And he liked the food at a place called Boston Pizza. Finally, I caved. I broke out of my routine and said yes.

With a population of about 400,000, Edmonton was just over half the size it is now, but it had vibrant pockets where Greek, Italian, and Chinese restaurants gave off a welcoming glow that drew a rowdy late-night crowd. And, of course, police officers. The owners of these places actually liked to see a couple of squad cars pull up after midnight. To this day I'm not sure why I have such a vivid memory of my first visit to the restaurant. I had been to literally hundreds of restaurants in all my years of being a police officer, from Regina to Prince George, and dozens of small towns in northern BC and Alberta in between.

If the Boston Pizza was nondescript outside, inside

it was nothing special either: an open kitchen and take-out counter by the front door, a few Greek statues in little alcoves circling a medium-sized dining area dotted with round tables, each covered in red oilcloth. For ambience, there was a picture of a volcano on the far wall. Another wall was covered in faux stone slabs. The decor was Greek, the food Italian, the name American and the waiters didn't really speak English. I didn't have high hopes for the food.

Even at that hour, the place was jumping. I was a plain-clothes police officer, sporting a longish haircut and a Fu Manchu moustache. There were two Boston Pizza locations—corporately owned stores—in Edmonton at the time, both owned and managed by the five Agioritis brothers: Trifon, Perry, Nino, George and Gus, the boss.

That night Perry greeted me, pencil in hand, yelling, "What do you want?"

I stared at the strange menu. I had no idea. What *did* I want? Back then the restaurant had 21 kinds of pizza and 3 kinds of pasta—no salads, no soup, no alcohol, just coffee and soft drinks. I didn't eat this kind of food, and I certainly didn't know how to order it.

Finally, Perry made a suggestion.

"Get the Hawaiian."

"Okay, sounds good."

The pizza arrived on a stiff piece of cardboard. It was a steaming circle of dough and sauce with some stuff on top held together with cheese. There were no utensils, just napkins. Perry motioned for me to pull the circle of dough apart—with my bare hands! I noticed it was cut into triangles. So I did, reluctantly. Then I took a bite—and it was good. The ham combined with the pineapple was different from anything this meat-and-potatoes Prairie boy had ever eaten, and I liked it. The meal was easy, fast and kind of fun. Pizza was the kind of thing you could put down in the middle of the table and share with friends, everyone grabbing a slice, which to me seemed exotic. In the Canada I grew up in, you sat silently at a table, the only noise being the scraping of your knife on the plate. I was an instant fan.

A few nights later, I found myself at the other location, this time picking up late-night takeout after raving about pizza to my wife. While I was waiting for the order, a fight broke out in the back. Without even thinking, I went into police mode, separating the guys fighting, grabbing them by the scruffs of their necks and tossing them both out. Nino, one of the Agioritis brothers, came over to thank me and offered me a job on the spot as a nighttime bouncer. Moonlighting in the RCMP wasn't allowed, so I just laughed and turned down the offer. "How about if you came in on Friday nights and ate for free—and stayed a while," he suggested. Seems the brothers had been having trouble with drunk university students getting rowdy, and they wanted to maintain the atmosphere of a family restaurant in a residential neighbourhood. If things got out of hand, Nino said, I'd just be a concerned citizen lending a hand. How could I turn down that offer? I loved the food, and the Agioritis brothers were a TV show in themselves, running around, cooking, cleaning, yelling, fighting and laughing. I sensed that they were my kind of people, loud, loving and gregarious.

So every Friday night, while Elaine worked a night shift at the hospital, I went to Boston Pizza and sipped a soft drink, waiting for a scrap to break out. And I didn't have to wait long. Any time you combine drunk students, pretty girls and the wee hours of the morning, you'll be sure to get a fight. So I was kept busy.

Those few months spent as an undercover bouncer at Boston Pizza were a lot of fun. Sometimes Don joined me. After closing the restaurant for the night, Nino would host an epic poker match at his apartment. (You found the place by looking for the long row of black pointy shoes beside the front door.) I spent a lot of time with the brothers, Gus in particular, the brother who started it all when he jumped ship in Vancouver Harbour in 1958, only $26 in his pocket. I once asked him why a Greek called his first restaurant *Boston* Pizza. He had never been to the city, and Edmonton was pretty much clear across the continent. He said you had to list three choices when registering a business with the city. He chose Parthenon Pizza, named after the Greek monument, and Santorini Pizza, after his home island, as backups. His first choice was Boston Pizza, after the city of Boston. Why Boston? He was a hockey fan, and he loved Bobby Orr, a Canadian who'd been recruited by the Boston Bruins as a teenager. Plus he liked the sound of the city: it felt solid, traditional, working class. So Boston Pizza it was. (I suspect the name was also easy for him to pronounce.)

Gus knew I was a police officer, and because he was at that time in the country illegally, he was cautious about me at first. Finally I convinced him that I could actually help him get his citizenship. I knew Boston Pizza operated on a cash-only basis, and I told him that if he got caught, all his success would be for nothing. But Gus didn't trust banks. He kept all his dough (the green kind) in a box hidden in a hole in the wall behind a picture in his office. Seriously. My table by the kitchen was a great spot from which to watch all the money pour into the restaurant. Truth be told, Gus never told me exactly how much the business made, even when we signed the formal franchise agreement. To Gus, if the drawer was full of cash and the customers were lining up, business was good. That was the extent of his business plan.

I did a bit of research and learned that there was an amnesty in effect; anyone in the country illegally had only to get a lawyer, fill out some forms and they'd be legal—no questions asked. It didn't take long to get it sorted out for him. Now legitimate, Gus could approach banks for loans to expand his business if he wanted. This was a crucial step, and Gus had to trust me in order for him to take it.

If You're Trudging, It's Time for Change

Don and I didn't need MBAs to know that Boston Pizza did a healthy business. And it was easy to see why. Pizza and pasta are mostly made from two ingredients: flour and water. One of those ingredients was extremely cheap, the other practically free, making food costs really low. (That's still the case today, which explains in part why there's a waiting list to become a Boston Pizza franchisee.)

Around the time I became a fixture at Boston Pizza, I also began to get frustrated with police work. The job was becoming political, with officers spending more time jockeying for top spots in their regiments than busting criminals. I started to look around at other opportunities within the RCMP, but I couldn't find anyone doing what I wanted to be doing in 5, 10, 15 years. I wasn't aspiring. This is a crucial part of corporate culture that most businesses ignore or skip over. If employees aren't aspiring to greater heights, to the next rung up the ladder at that business, the employee pool becomes stagnant with bored, resentful people whose productivity will start to slowly limp along. If you've ever worked with unenthusiastic people, you'll know that it's as though the oxygen level in the office decreases every time they enter it. People start to trudge to work. Negativity creeps in and poisons the environment.

Then came the RCMP regimental ball, to which we all wore our Red Serge. This particular night was a combination retirement-promotion party for two men with long careers with the RCMP. One was retiring after 30 years on the force, the other was heading across the country to a new position. The first would receive a gold watch, the other a plaque. As the chief inspector handed out the gifts, he got their names wrong and didn't even notice. At the time, the rest of us all laughed about the mix-up. But later, at home, it hit me hard. I realized that not only was I replaceable, I was interchangeable. After 30 years of service, it must have felt like the ultimate slap in the face for your inspector to get your name wrong. I couldn't shake that night off, and I knew that I didn't want to be either one of those guys.

When I became a police officer, I was sure that it was a

cradle-to-grave commitment. No looking back. But after the regimental ball, I began to feel an itch. I wanted a change. That's what happens sometimes. You choose your university major, you leave home, you sign that contract, you make that first big professional commitment—and then you run into an old friend from high school. And what he or she is doing looks a lot better than what you've got going on. Suddenly, you start questioning your decision to become a lawyer, and you sabotage the bar exam by getting trashed with your buddies the night before.

Even during RCMP training I got the sense that not everyone was going to make it, or that not everyone *wanted* to make it. Some recruits up and quit when it became pretty apparent to them that police work wasn't their calling. This was a big revelation to me. I was raised to commit. The idea that you could switch horses midstream was entirely alien to me: once I signed on to become a police officer, that was it. I remember one recruit who put on his uniform, went out behind the stables and shot himself. God only knows why he couldn't just quit, get help and find another professional path. But a very small part of me understood that rigidity, that stubbornness. I could understand how hard it is sometimes to say, "Hey, I was wrong about this decision; this is not for me after all. I want to change my mind." You don't want to let people down. You don't want them to think that everything they thought they knew about you was wrong.

Then came the clincher. I went to work one day to learn I was being transferred. Bad enough it was out east, to Ontario, but worse, I was being sent to a desk job. The RCMP had me in mind for a training position that would involve more paperwork: more forms and less actual police work. It hit me like a brick, because there was no discussion back then. They put you where they needed you, and you couldn't say no. The news caused every last ounce of remaining enthusiasm I had for the job to finally leak out of me.

At the same time, I had begun to realize how enthusiastic I was about my Friday nights at Boston Pizza. I began to really pay attention to what Gus and his brothers actually *did* for work. I noticed what kind of hours they kept, and asked myself, could I do that? I watched them at their tasks, again asking myself, do you think you could master that? Serve customers? Flip the dough? Make a giant vat of sauce? The day-to-day business of running a restaurant began to take over my thoughts, just as what life as a police officer would be like had done when I was going through basic training.

Imagining myself as a police officer was one of the key things that had kept me going. I had never paid attention to what Gus and his brothers wore to work, or what kind of shoes were required, but now I did. I listened to how they talked to their employees and what was expected of them. Boston Pizza had a family atmosphere and one of camaraderie—you could just feel it in the air. It attracted young students, the post-concert crowds, and busy families; people who liked its informality and the way you gathered around and shared a pizza. Remember, this was considered exotic—your meal plopped in the middle of the table, and reaching for it with your hands. But young people love to try new foods, and Canada was a young country. In the early 1960s, there were 8 million people (about 42% of the population) under the age of 19.

The switchover was almost involuntary, as though my heart "knew" before my head that I was about to make another big decision about my future. And, ultimately, it *was* a decision that took place in my heart. If I had left the decision to my head, it would have told me I was crazy to leave steady, pensioned pay for something so irregular and unsteady. But money wasn't the draw. The work, the culture, the possibilities were. For me, the restaurant had all the qualities I loved about police work: camaraderie, spontaneity and even shift work and odd hours. In my heart I knew I was leaving one calling for another—a simple decision, yet the hardest one I'd made so far. But I wasn't going to make that decision alone.

By then, Don Spence had also become disillusioned with police work. We both knew that if we stuck together, we could do well in the business. We had the personalities to draw and manage crowds, and we could learn to tackle the simple recipes that went into making great pizza and pasta dishes. The more we hung out at Boston Pizza with the Agioritis brothers, imagining that kind of life for ourselves, the more real it became. Our social lives had begun to revolve around Boston Pizza. And not for the first time, Gus suggested that I'd make a good pizza man. He recognized something in me before I did. I had the personality for this kind of work, Gus said. But as much as I could imagine working at Boston Pizza, and maybe even running one of my own, I still couldn't quite wrap my head around the idea of leaving the RCMP. It was like letting go of a security blanket.

Meanwhile, Gus opened a third location in Edmonton, another corporate-owned store that one of the brothers managed. I got the feeling I was watching something grow, something that could be successful—it was kind of like running beside a slow-moving train that you know will speed up at any moment, so you'd better make the leap. Gus lacked formal business training, but he had a really important quality: he didn't doubt himself. He had a natural confidence that wasn't steeped in arrogance. And his philosophy was: *This is a good thing. Let's make more. Join me.*

Trust People with More Confidence in You Than You Have in Yourself

I was with Don on a particularly busy night at Boston Pizza when, out of the blue, I blurted out, "Wouldn't it be great to get into this business?"

Don looked me right in the eye and without hesitating said, "Yeah, it would. Let's do it!"

That was it. A decision was made. But every decision has to be followed by action, and so we got right to it. We interrupted Gus and his brothers counting money in the back office.

"Gus," I said, "what do you say if Don and I opened up one of these restaurants?"

Gus stood up and shook my hand. "Finally," he said.

He knew we had no experience in the restaurant business, let alone pizza- and pasta-making skills. But here's the thing: Gus liked us. Most important, Gus trusted us, which was a big deal, since this was going to be Boston Pizza's first formal franchise. Thankfully, Gus had more confidence in us than we had in ourselves.

The first decision we made was the location. All three Boston Pizza restaurants were in Edmonton. Don and I wanted to open ours in British Columbia, in the Interior, where we both knew people and loved the climate. But Gus hadn't really thought about what it meant for other people to "open a Boston Pizza" in another province where no one knew the Edmonton stores. We were years away from understanding what it was that we had that people loved. No one had even heard of the word "brand" or given much thought to the idea of consistency. We planned to do what the Agioritis brothers did in Edmonton, but what did that mean exactly?

Next, Gus hired a lawyer and we put together the first Boston Pizza franchise agreement, which mirrored the one Dairy Queen and Kentucky Fried Chicken had used. There were some conditions, the first being that we couldn't open another Alberta location. That was territory he and his brothers carved out for themselves. We were fine with that.

To define our territory, we took a map of BC, the kind you buy at the gas station, and photocopied it. Then we took a red pen and drew big circles around the interior of the province, stopping short of the Lower Mainland. That area, which included Vancouver, was reserved for one of Gus's brothers. The Interior was to be our territory, assuming we would grow beyond just the one franchise in Penticton. And trust me, we were not thinking that far ahead. At the time, I felt that if I could make a go of the one restaurant, I would be a satisfied man.

The second condition: We had to use Gus's recipes. No problem, except there were no real recipes back then, nothing measured, standardized and tested, or written down. Still, we'd figure that out later. (The closest we ever came to maintaining consistency was with the spice bags that were shipped by bus from Edmonton to Penticton once a week. One of the brothers, George, assembled all the spices used in the meat and tomato sauces and put them into plastic bags, which he secured with twist-ties. They weren't labelled, so you had to eyeball the bags and know which was for the meat sauce and which was for the tomato. Once, en route to Penticton, a box of the spice bags broke open in the bus's undercarriage, trailing the distinct scent of Greek oregano all the way through the Okanagan Valley.)

The third condition: We had to use Gus's systems. And, as with the recipes, there were no real systems, at least nothing you'd recognize as the formal way Boston Pizza did things. But we agreed anyway.

Then Gus came up with the franchise fee: $5,000 plus 10% of sales. It seemed fair at the time, but remember, we didn't know exactly how much money the business was making from three restaurants. This information might have been a sticking point for anyone else, but the entire enterprise was built on a foundation of friendship and loyalty. In other words, personal relations trumped formal arrangements. It was more a decision based on how I felt about Gus rather than just the business, and my gut—my instincts—were right about him.

It was time to give my formal notice to the RCMP. Elaine and I had our baby daughter, Cheryl, by then, so money was a real concern. Elaine backed my decisions, but not until she was certain I was making the right one.

She was holding the baby when she said, "Jim, are you sure you know what you're doing?"

"Yes. It's gonna be great. We're gonna be fine," I answered, hoping my enthusiasm hid any doubts I had. Security is a big deal to a new mother. And though police work was dangerous, the pay was steady, and having a pension and great benefits was important. You don't just leave a good employer like the RCMP without a lot of thought and consideration. Because once you've told them you're out, you're out.

It's a deadening experience, walking the halls of your workplace like a zombie, sitting at a desk and staring at the clock, waiting for five o'clock to roll around. Luckily, I didn't get to that point with the RCMP. I made the decision to leave just as my work was becoming a grind, just when I had begun to avoid answering the phone so I didn't have to be the one to open a new file. And I think that's the trick of it. Don't wait until things get so bad that you exit on poor terms. Don't wait until your employers are as happy to see you go as you are to get out of there.

My RCMP "out" day was in May 1967. Going into the

detachment that day, I was nervous, maybe a little numb. But I was keenly aware that it had been more fun coming into the RCMP than it was going out. That's also why I knew I was making the right decision to leave. I couldn't summon any more enthusiasm for police work—at least the kind I was doing. My heart had left the building ages ago and was already well into running a restaurant. I knocked on my commanding officer's door and was invited to enter and sit down. I didn't beat around the bush.

"I'm leaving the RCMP," I said. "I've decided to pursue another line of work."

"What line of work is that?"

"I'm . . . going to open a restaurant."

There was a pause, then my commanding officer said, "Okay, son. You know the routine. Clear out your desk and meet me in the conference room."

There I had an exit interview, and I handed over my files and cases. I was told to drop off my gun, search warrants, badge and uniforms on the way out. That was it. I was no longer Constable Treliving. I was just Jim, the soon-to-be pizza guy.

You Can't Control How Others React to Your Decisions

The full weight of my decision to quit the RCMP didn't hit me until I got to the parking lot with my box of personal belongings. I sat in my car, feeling numb from head to toe, my mind racing. My fellow officers were the only friends I had, and members stick together. They know sensitive things about each other. Once you're no longer in the RCMP, you're no longer invited to socialize because you can't really be trusted in the same way. You're now a civilian. Members would have to watch what they say around you. That's the kind of change that's most frightening: the inability to control how other people around you will react to your decisions. I had told some of my colleagues that I was thinking of quitting the RCMP, but they probably never really thought I'd do it—every police officer I knew talked about leaving the force, about how they'd do so much better on their own, if *they* ran things. What salaried worker doesn't fantasize out loud about running his or her own business? But I knew that once I made the decision, I was going to take action. And my pride was such that I wouldn't be able to turn back. If I couldn't make it as a pizza man, I could never go back to being a police officer. My life as I knew it was over. My future was murky. I had a wife and a baby. Was I nuts?

As I drove away from the detachment that day, I felt my "Linus blanket" slip away. It was time for me to become a decision maker. I was scared, yes. But I was okay that day. And I was okay the next day. And the day after that. No matter how many people tried to dissuade me, something kept propelling me forward. When I thought about my (still non-existent) restaurant in Penticton, I felt happy. Happy in a way few things ever made me feel. When you get that feeling and you can't shake it off, and criticism doesn't kill it, you've won half the battle. I searched for regrets, and still there weren't any. That's when I knew I had made the right decision, that it had truly been time for me to leave the force. I felt as though a spell had been broken.

Things moved fast after that. I needed a job, any job, to get through the next six months. I wouldn't be getting paid while training at Boston Pizza, and Don and I needed to figure out the rest of our financing in order to buy equipment for the new franchise. We couldn't afford to fly, so we took road trips, Gus, Don and I, to the BC Interior, scouting for the perfect location. It took a while, but we finally found a two-storey building, a former furniture store, with a big, empty basement, at 511 Main Street in Penticton.

"This is the place. This will do well for you," Gus said. He knew. All three of his locations in Edmonton were successful. He was like our personal divining rod.

We signed a lease for $600 a month. That was dirt cheap for such a big space, far less than what comparable places were leasing for in Kelowna. Now it was time to build our financial base.

Back in Edmonton, the next few months were a blur of making dough at odd hours, and working at even odder jobs. Life was unpredictable and exhausting, but exhilarating. I had a stint at Sears selling major appliances. I sold boats for a while at a marina, kept the books for City Spring and Welding and worked at the Corona Hotel as a bouncer, a place far tougher than Boston Pizza—anything to raise the money. I even enjoyed a brief stint as a pro wrestler.

The Osborne Brothers, Bud and Ray out of Edmonton, were big competitors of Stampede Wrestling, a wildly popular pro wrestling show at the time. I had met Bud at an autobody shop my wife's uncle owned. He was getting a hound's head welded onto the hood of his Cadillac to signify "top dog."

Bud took in my size.

"Big guy like you could make good money in the ring."

At first I just worked out with Bud and Ray at the local gym. They showed me how to toss around a medicine ball, then taught me a few holds and throws. Eventually, they pressed me into service, throwing a face mask at me for anonymity's sake.

"You're an ex-RCMP. You might get recognized."

My moniker was "Hangman." I made about $200 per match—a small fortune—and sometimes more if I won. Matches were rehearsed. Sometimes I was the heel (the loser), sometimes the crowbar (the winner). Razors were sewn into our gloves so we could strategically bleed ourselves during battle. It was a hoot, really—until I was thrown over the ropes in Barrhead, Alberta, and spent two weeks in the hospital with my leg elevated until the blood clot had dissolved. That's when Elaine laid down the law. No more wrestling, anything but wrestling. And so ended my brief career in the ring.

Tune Out Doubters

There was nothing I wouldn't try, nothing I wouldn't do, to make enough money to open that restaurant. I was that committed, that passionate. When an idea is fuelled by hunger and conviction, it grows muscles and stands a much better chance of working. Besides, my only thought was, what's the worse thing that could happen? That I'd land in the hospital? Done. I survived. That I'd get fired? That happened too. Big deal. There was always another job around the corner. No matter what, I always had a sense that this idea to open a Boston Pizza franchise was a winning idea. The business was growing, wasn't it? I wasn't buying blindly into a dream. I had spent hours and hours at Boston Pizza and at Gus's home. I played poker with him and got to know his family. His friends became my friends. Don's and my principles lined up with his. We wanted to make a good solid business out of the restaurant, and make enough money to pay people working wages and provide a good time for the folks who ate there. Our goals were simple and similar. And if Penticton worked out, we'd grow it somewhere else. We weren't doing this to drive fancy cars or to sock away wads of cash. We were looking for a new adventure. I always kept that in mind, even when doubts crept in, mine or other people's. One time, a force member saw me at Sears selling refrigerators. After taking in my cheap suit, he shook his head at me and asked with real concern, "Treliving? What the hell are you doing, buddy?"

"Just trying to scratch out a living," I said, shrugging. I tried to keep the attitude that those odd jobs were temporary, and for a greater cause. I'd remind myself that I was learning skills and meeting new people. I never sneered at any of the work I got or at any of the people I met along the way. I was grateful for every dime I earned during those months. Plus I always hoped I'd meet someone who might consider financing our dream, a silent partner, someone who didn't want to work in the pizza business themselves but had the money to back a couple of guys who did.

By day, Don and I also collected restaurant equipment—an oven or a stockpot here, a dough mixer there—storing it all in our garages until it was time to make the big move to Penticton. By night, we were learning how to run a restaurant. We did every job, from washing dishes to waiting tables to bussing and setting them. But the biggest adjustment was losing my "ice face" when working the front of the house. Friends pointed out that I was greeting customers like they were suspects. Without even realizing it, I'd be scoping them out, looking them up and down—so you can just imagine my expression. It's not something I could just shut off, but I've learned over the years to camouflage it with a smile. I've had lapses on *Dragons' Den,* when I'm so tuned in to a pitcher's body language, paying attention to where their eyes shift, how their feet shuffle, watching for evidence of deceit or exaggeration, that my "ice face" resurfaces; I see flashes of it when I watch the shows on TV. I don't apologize for it—it's a useful skill. But you can't show it at a restaurant.

Around the time I was training at Boston Pizza, my marriage with Elaine entered the stage that many entrepreneurs experience when they start out on a new venture. It's an all-consuming time, and though you tell yourself that it's for the greater good, for the family and its security, deep down you know it's not good for a marriage to just pass each other in the night. But that's what was beginning to happen. Elaine was busy with the baby, and I was busy building a business. If I wasn't at one of my various jobs, I was at Boston Pizza, training and learning. Time was ticking. But back then you didn't sit down and talk through things. Instead, you ploughed ahead and hoped for better times.

Gus charged his brother George with the task of teaching me how to cook the Boston Pizza way. Though I was a bad student in my teens, I was an avid student in my late 20s, hovering over a big pot of sauce while George walked me through the recipes. But as soon as the so-called training began, I knew I was in trouble. I can still see myself standing in that hot kitchen, wearing an apron, notebook in hand, eager to learn the ropes.

"Okay, George. Meat sauce. Show me how to make it. What goes into it?"

George looked at me sternly, his thick eyebrows raised.

"What's doze for?" he asked, pointing at my hands.

"It's a pen and a notebook, George. I wanna write everything down so we can duplicate the recipes."

"No. You doan need to write anyting-a down, Jeem. I no like."

"George, I gotta. How else am I going to make it exactly how you make it?"

"You gonna watch."

And off he went, throwing "a little-a bit a dis, and a little-a bit a dat" into a giant vat of simmering meat sauce. His hands were a blur, tossing a pinch of this herb and that spice into the pot, stirring all the while.

"That's how you make-a da meat sauce. You got it, Jeem?"

"I . . . think so."

For rolling out pizza dough, it was more of the same. I'd mimic George slapping at the warm dough.

"Like this?"

"No, Jeem, you go like-a dis." *Slap, slap, slap.* "Den you take-a dis hand and go like-a-dat. Den you pudda dis and pudda dat. Done."

"Done. So then it goes in the oven, right? For how long?"

"Until it looks-a like a dis," he'd say, proudly pulling out a piping hot pizza, its crust perfectly browned.

We paid $5,000 for "a little-a bit a dis, and a little-a bit a dat, you pudda the meat, you adda the onion, go like a-dat, do like a-dis." That was the extent of our Boston Pizza cooking lessons. Don and I would just have to wing the rules, recipes and regulations. And yet, we happily paid the franchise fee because there was still a Boston Pizza flavour and a certain feel to the place we knew we could duplicate. Today, all Boston Pizza recipes are standardized. We've perfected a flavour, and we replicate that taste in all our stores. But when I cook at home, I rarely use a measuring cup. I like to throw things together like George taught me—and, let me assure you, I'm a pretty good cook.

It was the middle of January 1968 when I loaded up a U-Haul with our restaurant equipment and hitched it to the back of my station wagon. I felt like a homesteader creeping along the snowy highway, crossing provincial lines. It was pretty treacherous driving, with a few memorable fishtails to keep me alert. Both Elaine and Don were staying behind in Edmonton until I got settled and took possession of the building that would house the restaurant. After another near-deadly spinout I saw red lights flashing behind me, beckoning me to pull over. Perfect, I thought. That's just what I need—an RCMP officer's lecture about safety. One more final humiliation before I got to Penticton. The officer took one look at my licence and registration and handed it back to me with a grin.

"Treliving, what the hell are you doing out here in the middle of nowhere with all this crap hitched to your car? And where in the hell are you going?"

It was Barry Hughes, a recruit I knew from RCMP training. I told him I had quit my job and was opening up a little pizza place in Penticton.

He shook his head and tipped his hat.

"You're out of your freaking mind, Jim," he said. "But good luck to you, man."

Truth be told, I had no real idea what lay ahead for us, or how hard the next two years were going to be and how close I'd come to financial disaster. And I consider that a blessing. In fact, if I had known all the pitfalls before hitching that U-Haul to my station wagon and *still* went ahead with it, the decision would have had more to do with insanity than courage. I did not know it at the time, but the next couple of years would test every entrepreneurial muscle I had.

By the way, Barry waived the ticket. I told him to come visit me and I'd buy him dinner. A few months later, he did. Eventually, he came to work for Boston Pizza, after I drove out to Kelowna to persuade him to join us. His wife wasn't a fan of the idea. She chased me out of the house with a hot iron that afternoon. But he became one of my closest friends—I caught the golf bug from him—and he eventually became Boston Pizza's chief contractor. In fact, he built Boston Pizza's venues for Expo '86, an event that secured the company's future. A few years later, Barry was killed by a drunk driver as he headed home from my 50th birthday party. I'll never forget his goodbye to me that night. It was the first time he had ever hugged me. He was halfway down the driveway when he turned and ran back. "Big!" he said—that was his nickname for me. "We made it to 50. Can you believe it?" He was dead an hour later, a tragedy I've never really gotten over.

It was five o'clock in the afternoon when I rolled into Penticton and parked my car and trailer in front of my Uncle Jack's place. He and my Aunt Edna were putting me up for the next few months, until I got a place of my own. Now the real work would begin. Not the building, not the cooking, cleaning or serving. That was nothing. The hardest part about starting a business, as anyone who's ever appeared on *Dragons' Den* will attest to, is finding the money to finance your dream. That's the whole premise of the TV show, and it's the essence of entrepreneurship—raising capital. Don and I had some money, but we'd need a lot more. I had big plans for that giant empty basement below the restaurant. I even had a name for it: Boston's Bottom. A nightclub wasn't part of the deal with Gus, but it became a crucial financial support when, a year later, we found ourselves waist deep in debt and desperately looking for help from a young accountant named George Melville.

Checklist for Becoming a Decision Maker

Leaving a sure thing for a big maybe was one of the biggest decisions I'd ever made in my life. It was a total life change. But I felt I had no choice. I was a young man. I had just begun to understand myself—and I wanted to have more control over my life. I wanted to become a decision maker, an entrepreneur. How do I know a big decision needs to be made? When I no longer feel effective, when, despite all efforts on my part, I can't seem to make a bad situation better. Here are a few other tips that can guide you in making a big decision:

1. Surround Yourself with People Who Want You to Succeed. This is tricky. Sometimes people with bad ideas continue down a destructive path because they're surrounded by people who tell them only what they want to hear. That's not what I'm talking about. If a big decision has passed your head, heart and gut test, and you know you're on the right path, you have to tune out the naysayers. As happy as some of my fellow officers were for me when I told them I was leaving the force, many weren't. Some tried talking me out of it. Some dropped subtle hints that I might not be cut out for the work of running a restaurant. Maybe it was jealousy, I don't know. But it's a crucial stage when you've made a big decision. I've come to realize the fundamental importance of surrounding yourself with people who genuinely want you to succeed. They can oftentimes carry your enthusiasm for you in those moments when it all gets to be too much.

2. A Decision Isn't an Action; It's Just a Decision. Think of the old adage about three birds sitting on a wire. One makes the decision to fly away. How many birds are left? Lots of people answer "two," but it's actually three. The bird made only a decision. The point is, get cracking. This goes back to my police training. Always do something.

3. Develop Stamina. I lost count of the number of jobs I held between the time I left the RCMP and when I moved to Penticton. The goal was to make as much money as possible, but I was also cultivating important entrepreneurial muscles because I was constantly making decisions, then revising them. I was learning about flexibility and resilience. I was learning to set goals and then execute them. I was learning how to manage my time and maintain momentum. After all, the worst decision you can make in difficult times is no decision. And the worst thing you can do after making a big decision such as changing careers or moving to a new city is to sit around and think about it. You've made the decision, so take the action, then move on to the next decision and the action after that.

4. Assume You'll Second-Guess Big Decisions. My first big decision was to become an RCMP officer. I thought it would be the last big decision I'd make about my life. But that decision set into motion a series of events, until

I made the leap into an entirely different field. Now I never think of my decisions as final ones. They simply send me in a certain direction with a lot of momentum. If things turn out, it doesn't necessarily mean it was the right decision. And if things don't turn out as planned, it means I have to get in front of the dilemma and make yet another decision, followed by more action. It's a relentless life, being an entrepreneur. It's also really rewarding. But it's not for everyone.

5. Don't Count on Consensus. It's nice when consensus happens, when everyone's on the same page. But it may never come. Here's the thing: a decision maker makes a decision and then takes responsibility for the outcome, especially if it's a bad one. However, if it's a good outcome, you shouldn't take the credit. Sounds tough, but that's how I feel. In my partnerships, I've always strived for consensus. Sometimes we reach it. Sometimes we don't. But at the end of the day, when a decision must be made, it's made.

4

HOW WILL I FUND MY DREAM?

Making Crucial Financial Decisions

"Creditors have better memories than debtors."
—Benjamin Franklin

Never Confuse Seeking Help with Seeking Approval

Usually the question isn't whether or not to borrow money to build your dream. Rather, the question is how much will you borrow and from whom? And most important, how will you pay it back? Opening a restaurant is expensive. In 1968, we were looking at about $23,000 to get the whole thing up and running. In about a 10-month period, between leaving the RCMP and packing the car for Penticton, I think I managed to put together $5,000—an incredible amount of money in such a short period, especially with a wife and baby to support.

Don and I had paid the $5,000 franchise fee to Gus out of our pension buyouts. But where would we get the rest? The only person I knew who had that kind of money was my dad, and that conversation was one I had delayed as long as possible. "Hi, Dad! I'm thinking of leaving a well-paying, highly respected, secure government job to open up a pizza place, a business I've never worked in before. Can you lend me some money?" I couldn't imagine a good outcome.

Five thousand dollars is nothing to sneeze at today, but it was a heck of a lot of money back then. And we needed it. Just before the big move to Penticton, I made a crucial visit home to Virden. I couldn't delay the conversation with my dad a minute longer. This was not a request I could make over the phone. I had to see him in person. I was hoping my dad would see in me the potential to be a great entrepreneur. But when I contemplated heading to Virden to finally break the news to him, to tell him I had left the RCMP for a life in restaurants, I reverted back to being a kid. Here I was a grown man, with a wife, child and new business, but I still needed my dad's approval, not to mention that $5,000 loan. That was the hard step I took en route to building my business. Why? Because making money for people is a terrific privilege; paying people money you owe them is a solemn act. I have always considered it a breach of my principles to carry debt too far, let alone not pay back a loan. I couldn't imagine not paying my dad back—and yet, I knew there was a risk, however small, that this could happen. And I knew he would know it too.

An uncle of mine was a safety supervisor for a transport company in Edmonton, and he let me hitch a ride with one of his drivers back to Manitoba. After 22 hours of driving, he dropped me off at a gas station near Virden, from where I called my mother to pick me up. On the way to the house, I gave her the short version of the story. I had left the RCMP. I was working a series of odd jobs to put together enough money to open a restaurant in a city I'd never lived in before. Oh, and by the way, Elaine was working full time as a nurse to support us, leaving Cheryl with a babysitter. I was living a life exactly the opposite of my father's and contrary to how I'd been raised. I wondered if my mother thought about the time my dad made her quit the job she held for all of two hours. She was pregnant a few months later with my sister Pat, who was now a pretty 11-year-old greeting me at the door of my childhood home. My sister Joy, who was three years younger than me, had just got married.

If my mother was shocked or dismayed by my plans, she didn't say anything. But my dad could tell I was home for more than just a quick visit, and I could tell he wasn't going to make it easy on me, whatever he thought I was there to do. After I dropped off my bag in my old room, I met my dad at the dining-room table and came right out with it. I told him I had left the force and that I was home to borrow some money for a new business. Making pizza.

"I see."

"It's a great business opportunity. These restaurants are doing gangbusters in Edmonton, Dad, and a partner and I, we want to open the very first franchise in Penticton."

My dad was quiet for a second and then he said, "Let me get this straight, Jim. You left a secure job to get into business with a Greek guy who makes Italian food for a restaurant that has an American name in a Canadian city?"

"Yes."

"What do you know about pizza?" He pronounced it *PEE-zah*, not *PEET-zah*.

"Well, I know a lot about it."

"Why? Because you hang around a peeza shop drinking coffee?"

He had a point, but I persevered. "It's a sure thing, Dad," I said. "We've got the money for the franchise fee, and we've already bought the equipment. Five thousand dollars is the last bit of money we need to really make a go of it. I just need a hand."

"You don't need a hand, Jim, you need a psychiatrist."

It was a real insult back in those days for people to say there was something wrong with your head. And with that my dad got up from the table and said goodnight. After he left, I begged my mother to talk to him, to try to persuade him that my idea was a good one. She said she'd do what she could, but we both knew my dad. We both knew he kept his own counsel where money was concerned. He made financial decisions rationally, not emotionally. And here I was hoping to appeal to his heart about the matter. I was his son, after all.

I spent a sleepless night staring at the ceiling of my bedroom. My dad was smart. And my dad knew me. And although he loved me, he knew I struggled with the concept of discipline, which is why he was so happy that I had entered the RCMP. Maybe there I would learn discipline, the one thing I seemed to lack, in his eyes. For my dad, decisions about money were always made with his head and informed by discipline—which you needed in order to borrow the right amount and pay it back in a timely fashion.

By the time I got up for breakfast, my dad had already left for work. Not a good sign. That likely meant he was mad at me. I was pouting and trying to figure out how I was going to get back to Edmonton when the phone rang. My mother answered it, murmured a few words and hung up.

"That was Mr. Dumpleton at the bank. Clean yourself up, Jim, and go down and meet him there. Your dad's going to co-sign a loan for you."

It was a revered place, the bank manager's office. I'll never forget the large picture of the young Queen hanging behind his head, or the dark-panelled walls topped with fogged glass. His reading glasses sat low on his nose as he motioned for me to sit down in a deep, leather chair.

"Hello, Jim. Your dad came by this morning and mentioned to me that you're getting into a business of some kind. Involving restaurants."

"Yes, sir, that's right. We're opening a pizza franchise in the Okanagan."

"Right."

Mr. Dumpleton made no further comment, but his stern look said it all. He cleared his throat and explained that my father had agreed to co-sign a loan for $5,000, which I was to repay over five years.

"I'm only going to say this once, Jim. Do not miss a payment. I don't want to go after your dad for the money. And if you miss a payment, that's where I'll be heading. You understand?"

There I was, a former police officer who'd solved complicated murders, apprehended dangerous suspects and sat in on gruesome autopsies, a guy who weighed 220 pounds (which shot up to 250 during our first year in the pizza business), feeling intimidated by a skinny banker wearing spectacles.

"Don't worry, Mr. Dumpleton, I won't miss a payment. I promise."

In a way, the best thing my dad could have ever done for me was to move that loan over to the bank. I always caution entrepreneurs about borrowing money from family and friends. I don't dissuade them, but I do caution them. Money can destroy relationships, and nothing's more corrosive than an unpaid debt between family members.

Still, when I stood up and shook Mr. Dumpleton's hand enthusiastically, I was keenly aware that it wasn't my business idea that secured the loan. It wasn't even my enthusiasm. What got me that money, plain and simple, was the personal relationship my dad had with Mr. Dumpleton. Although my father would agree that I was an honest and hard-working young man, we both knew I lacked natural discipline. And I was getting into a business I knew nothing about. Having a bank front the loan was added insurance for him that I would pay it back. Bad enough that I should miss a payment to my dad, but the idea that I would embarrass him further in front of Mr. Dumpleton was unthinkable. My dad knew that about me. My lack of discipline was always trumped by my loyalty, my word.

For the next two years, I was often late paying other bills, sometimes even skipping them altogether, in order to make that one monthly payment. It was much later that I learned there had never really been a loan: my dad had arranged with Mr. Dumpleton to deposit $5,000 into an account for me. Mr. Dumpleton was merely the front. I had been directly paying my dad back the whole time.

Sometimes You Have to Break the Rules to Break Even

Elaine and our baby daughter, Cheryl, joined me in Penticton, but until the restaurant was up and running and we could pay ourselves a living wage, Don had kept his job with the Edmonton police. In those months before we opened, money was as tight as it had ever been, and I helped where I could with the construction of the restaurant. Don and I had decided to open the restaurant and the nightclub at the same time, which at first might have seemed foolish, since the nightclub sucked up all of our money and any cushion we might have needed. But in the long run it turned out to be a life-saving decision financially.

We knew how much it would cost to build just the restaurant. The nightclub was going to be another $90,000, a huge amount of money, way more than we had. So we did what a lot of small businesses do: we made appointments with banks—all of them—to ask for a loan. And one by one they turned us down. We ended up at the Industrial

Development Bank—the last stop for entrepreneurs in search of cash. There Don and I sat down in yet another dark-brown office while a loan officer explained that, to qualify, we had to have been rejected by at least three other banks.

"Is that all?" I said. "We've got more rejections than that."

Miraculously, the bank gave us $50,000, enough to complete construction on the basement and begin making payments to the contractors.

The last thing on our to-do list was getting the liquor licence. For that, we had to drive all the way to Victoria for a hearing, and along with us came everyone in Penticton who objected to Boston's Bottom, which is what we were planning to call the nightclub. Every church, including my own, had signed a petition, as did the parents of kids who went to the high school a few blocks from the restaurant. I watched as a very large woman slowly made her way to the front of the courtroom, accompanied by her wisp of a husband. She launched into a fire-and-brimstone speech about drunks all going to hell. Heading the hearing was Colonel Donald McGugan, the legendary head of the BC Liquor Control Board and a man known to enjoy a Scotch or two at lunch.

Finally having had enough of the woman's sermon, the colonel turned to Don and me and said, "Gentleman, I have one question and one condition. My question is, do you two know a real drunk when you see one?"

"Yes, sir, we do," I replied.

"How do you come by this knowledge?"

"Well, I was an RCMP officer stationed in Prince George for a number of years. My partner was an Edmonton city police officer. We know our drunks quite well."

He contemplated my answer for a moment.

"Fine. I'll grant you your liquor licence. But here's the condition: No singing at this establishment. It's to be quiet."

We looked at each other and shrugged.

"Sure. Absolutely. No singing."

On May 10, 1968, we opened our doors. Boston Pizza, Penticton, was packed on opening weekend and it didn't let up all summer. And although the food was a little inconsistent (sometimes Don made the sauce, sometimes I did, sometimes we used the right spice bag, sometimes we got them mixed up), we started to get regular customers, and we had a nice nightclub business going on down in the basement.

Now, the nightclub was not part of the original plan. In fact, for a long time, Gus didn't even know about Boston's Bottom. Our agreement was to pay him the franchise fee from the profits earned in the restaurant, from food sales only. We broke the rules a little, but we had no idea how much we'd come to rely on liquor sales for revenue those first few years of business. Keep in mind that a nightclub is different from a bar. Boston's Bottom offered live entertainment and dancing, not found today in a Boston Pizza, where you can grab a drink and watch the game at the bar. And, yes, we had told the colonel there'd be no singing.

We soon discovered the biggest problem with running a nightclub. Despite cover charges and great margins on booze, it isn't very cost-effective. If you're a hit, you can make money end over end, but only for a short period. That's because every 18 months or so, you have to renovate and reinvent the nightclub's concept. A nightclub's big selling points are booze and ambience, and the only thing you really have any control over is the ambience. That means new decor, new carpeting, and sometimes a new name. It's not just because of the wear and tear from all the drinking and dancing and fighting. Nightclubs go out of style. Plus live bands cost a lot of money—the good ones, anyway. We often booked a band called The Great Canadian River Race that was so raucous they had patrons jumping up to punch holes in the ceiling at the end of the night when they sang "Jeremiah Was a Bullfrog." But they brought in a young crowd, including a kid named Mike Rynoski, who used to hang out in the restaurant, his mother often calling to tell me to send him home. You might know him better as Mike Reno, the lead singer of Loverboy.

By building Boston's Bottom, we weren't deliberately trying to enhance the brand or to pull one over on Gus. We were only hoping to make a buck, any and every way possible. And for a while, Boston's Bottom was *the* place to be on Friday and Saturday nights, and I loved being at the centre of it all. It was a jarring transition—going from the organized machine of the RCMP to the borderline chaos of running a restaurant and nightclub—but I thrived in both environments. As I've said, I have that kind of personality. I love to be where the action is. And you can't be more in the middle of things than when you're the proprietor of the hottest nightclub—the first nightclub—in the Okanagan Valley. That first summer in business there was one of the best, and busiest, of my life.

Then came September.

The contrast between the hustle of a hot August night in a busy restaurant and the quiet of September was stark. And when I say business died in September, I mean it was taken behind the barn and shot. Just as the crowds began to dwindle, our financial problems began to appear. But since we were the first Boston Pizza franchise, we had nothing to compare our operating costs to.

Construction on the nightclub had also gone way over budget, but we thought we had the numbers straight. And although Don and I were the chief cooks and bottle washers, we did have to hire full-time staff. A waitress named Betty Green followed us from Edmonton, and Elaine helped out on the weekends when she wasn't at the hospital, sometimes leaving Cheryl, now a toddler, colouring at one of the tables while she served customers. Elaine was also pregnant with our son, Brad, at the time, and some nights we raided the restaurant's fridge to bring home milk and eggs to eat.

I soon began to realize that we were doing something horribly wrong with our accounting. Don and I couldn't figure out how we were bringing in all that money but bleeding it out just as quickly. Sales from the nightclub were good and should have helped us support the restaurant upstairs during the months the tourists left town. That had been the plan, and it was a good one. But we were dead broke by Christmas, and our creditors came a-knocking. All we needed was to miss one payment and a contractor could put a lien on our establishment. A lien meant no liquor licence, no liquor licence meant no nightclub, no nightclub meant no Boston Pizza, no Boston Pizza meant no 10% franchise fee to Gus and that meant we'd be cooked.

Never Take the Back Door

We finally took our broke selves over to the only accounting firm in town, Peat Marwick, the precursor to KPMG. There we met a young, recent graduate (and newlywed) by the name of George Melville, who took a long look at our ledger. Then he said he'd come by the restaurant the next day with a student and start sorting through our financials. We set them up at a card table on the dance floor under the cleaning lights in Boston's Bottom. While the adding machine clacked away downstairs, I served tables and wiped my sweaty brow, waiting for the verdict as if George were a doctor about to deliver bad news.

After a few days, he finally gave it to us straight.

"Don, Jim, you're in trouble. You have a mess on your hands here. You have no long-term financing in place, you have a lot of different creditors, you're undercapitalized and you've got into the bad habit of borrowing from Peter to pay Paul."

The biggest mistake we had made was with our schedule of payments. We'd get a bill and pay it in full. Another bill would come in and we'd pay that in full too. I thought that's what you were supposed to do. Problem was, we weren't coordinating our payment cycles to match the rhythm of our business. And it never occurred to us to adjust our schedule of payments to see if we could pay smaller amounts over a longer period for a slightly higher rate.

I was also beginning to experience a creeping sense of panic every time I saw one of the contractors we owed come by the restaurant. And I didn't want to be *that* guy, the one who hid from people he owed money to, who slinked out the back door and down the alley instead of taking the front door and the sidewalk. That's not who I was raised to be.

I remembered a saying of my dad's: Anyone can hire an accountant, but not everyone's willing to listen to him. In a crisis, it boils down to two simple questions: Are you willing to accept help? And are you willing to make the changes suggested? Most people in trouble are not operating with an open mind. Instead of being flexible to suggestions, they shut down and become even more entrenched. Luckily, Don and I were always on the same page. We had surrendered. We were willing to listen to every suggestion George made now that we had hit those unmistakable financial roadblocks.

"Let's invite the creditors over. Let's tell them everything," I said to George. After all, if you can't give your creditors the money right away, you have to give them something else to put them at ease: information.

Three days later, a stream of men entered the restaurant an hour before the supper rush and quietly filed downstairs to the nightclub. There were the guys from Oscar

Sather Flooring, contractors from Clark and Eschelman, and Barney Bent from Pacific Pipe and Flume. Every one of them had busted their butts to get the restaurant and nightclub finished and opened on time, and I owed every one of them a lot of money.

I began the presentation bluntly.

"I want to pay you back, but I don't have the money right now."

The room filled with groans, hats came off, heads were scratched, feet were shuffled, more beer was poured. George handed out papers documenting in black and white our financials.

"This is what Don and I have coming in and out, every month, summer and winter. Going forward we're going to do monthly budgets. Copies will be sent to your offices. You will see all the money coming in and out of this place. You will get a certain percentage of the profits every month, when there are profits. Most important, you will be paid before we get paid. But cheques will only come at the end of summer. Through the winter, no one can get paid because the restaurant won't bring in enough revenue, and it has to stay afloat. But come summer, the money will flow again. If you're patient and don't put a lien on this place, it should take about three years. But you'll all get the money you're owed, every last one of you. I promise. We got in over our heads. I apologize. And we had no idea that the revenue would drop off so steeply in the fall. I don't blame any of you if you put a lien on this place. If you do that, you will get your money faster, but only some of you will get your money back. But I promise you this: with this plan, you will *all* get paid, but only if they don't close us down. I also promise you're not going to see Don or me driving a fancy car, or living in a big house, or going on vacation, or spending any significant amount of money until you all get paid what we owe you."

That was my speech. No one was thrilled, but no one put a lien on the restaurant and nightclub. Every one of those contractors hung on for the entire three years, during which time Don and I shared a vehicle, my wife worked weekends for free and I pulled 20-hour shifts. In the end, every one of our creditors was paid back. And we made the payments with a little pomp and ceremony. Every September we made reservations for a couple dozen at the fanciest restaurant in town, the Purple Steer. Our creditors put on clean shirts for the occasion. Beneath each of their plates was a big, fat cheque. Everyone ordered the most expensive thing on the menu and got rip-roaring drunk, and we picked up the tab.

Some of these guys became great regulars at Boston Pizza, some lifelong friends. Those relationships were forged from making the smartest decision in our young entrepreneurial careers: when dogged by debt, choose transparency. Imagine if this kind of policy was employed more widely, and not just in business but in politics too. Imagine how much more agency people would feel. Because creditors just want to get paid. And often it's not financial insecurity that's the problem but the fear of it. Transparency alleviates fear. People can relax. Business gets done.

Critical Skills Are Cultivated under Fire

I want to revisit the first critical decision we made, which landed us on the brink of financial crises to begin with: choosing Penticton. Kelowna was our first pick, but it was a sleepy town year-round and we didn't know a soul there, whereas I had family in Penticton. When we first visited Penticton in the late summer prior to building, it looked like a winner. The town was busy. The streets were bustling and the crowds were young and lively. Most important, rent was cheap. We calculated that we could afford to pay rent even if we weren't packing the place night after night. Kelowna's rent would have wiped us out if we had even one bad month. So you might think I'd look back on Penticton as the first bad decision we made.

You'd be wrong. I learned that financing can be flexible, and that people just want their money back in a timely fashion—and everyone defines "timely" differently. I learned that having a personal relationship with your employees and customers is as important as cultivating one with your creditors. I learned not to be afraid of banks. After all, they make money off people like me. Also, during the slow times, we didn't sit around; we diversified, built up the nightclub business and I took on side projects like concert promoting. I formed a company called Playmor Productions with Bob Harris, the young manager of The Great Canadian River Race. Don resented the time I spent away from the restaurant booking bands into local arenas—until I started carting back briefcases with thousands of dollars stuffed inside. I always split the profits with him. We were partners, after all.

But the most critical decision we made was opening the nightclub to begin with. It wasn't part of the original plan, but that nightclub kept us afloat. And it provided a crash course in running an entertainment venue in its entirety, I mean every aspect of it, from the kitchen to the nightclub to the entertainment. Our apologies to Colonel McGugan, but we did, in fact, allow singing, because you do what you need to do to stay afloat. And singers brought in the crowds.

The other benefit Penticton provided was that it was built on the other side of a mountain range from Edmonton, and that mountain range served as a geographical shield between us and Gus. He just didn't venture over the mountains much to check on his BC franchise. So we could get away with doing whatever it took to stay in business. We had to. We tweaked with the menu and the recipes, challenging the boundaries of our fairly loose franchise agreement. We introduced a salami, cheese, pepperoni and onion sandwich called the "Boston Brute" that was a big hit. It required fewer ingredients than pizza, so margins were good. We raised prices without consulting him. We also became really aware of what franchisees need: on-the-ground support, consistency, a clear marketing plan. We didn't have any of those things, but you better believe they're at the root of our business now. Plus there were signs—odd signs—that told me I was in the right place, doing the right thing, with the right people. For instance, whenever I needed money, and I mean *needed* money, the exact amount always appeared somehow.

Once, when we were on the brink of missing a rent payment by a couple hundred dollars, my uncle just happened to mail me a cheque for the exact sum we needed to cover it. I know there's big business in convincing people that, in order to get something, it's enough to just really, really want it. I don't believe that stuff myself, but sometimes the universe does send you a sign that you're on the right track. And this kept happening to me.

Another time, at the end of our first winter in business, I came to realize that there was no way I was going to make payroll for that Friday. I needed $4,000. In fact, I knew in my heart that we were cooked, done, a few days away from shutting the doors for good. I felt a sense of resignation, but I also felt that we had really given it our all. We had tried, but there was just no way I was going to come up with that much money in only four days. Then, as if right out of some western, a stranger darkened the doorway of Boston Pizza. No word of a lie: I remember it was high noon on Main Street and the restaurant was open for lunch but completely empty.

Turns out he was no stranger but a man named Les Edgelow, a former police officer turned Pepsi rep who had come by for a bite.

"Treliving! It *is* you! I heard you opened a place here."

It was so good to see a friendly face, especially in those dark days. I gave him a big slap on the back and pulled out a chair for him. He looked around at our fine little establishment and asked me how I was doing.

"Great, great," I lied. "Business is booming." I felt like I was Scarlett O'Hara, getting all dolled up in an effort to convince Rhett Butler things were going grand for her after the war. She was after him for cash, and she knew he wouldn't give money to a failing venture. No way was I going to tell Les that business was dying, that I couldn't make payroll and that we were days away from calling this whole thing a big, fat failure.

Les became distracted by the glowing sign over the soda fountain.

"Jim, why are you with Coke?"

I shrugged. "I don't know. The Coke rep was here first." There had been no big pitch, no big deliberation, nothing like the dance that goes into aligning yourself with brands today. The Coke guy really had been there first.

"What'll it take for you to switch over to Pepsi?" Les asked.

I told him I still owed Coca-Cola for the dispenser and refrigerators. I couldn't just tear them out and put in Pepsi equipment without paying Coke off first.

"How much do you still owe?"

"About $4,000," I said. This was true; that was how much it would cost for me to pay off Coca-Cola, remove its equipment, and switch over to Pepsi.

"I'll pay it," said Les. "Let me write you a cheque right now for $4,000, and I'll pop off that Coke sign and put in Pepsi. I'll bring the rest of the equipment tomorrow."

So Les Edgelow wrote me a cheque for $4,000. I stared at it after he left. It had happened again. Money I needed had fallen into my lap. The exact amount, in fact. I was able to make payroll that Friday, and the Coke bill wasn't due for 90 days. By then, the summer crowds would be packing the place again. Our first year, the restaurant did $52,000 in sales; Boston's Bottom did about $75,000. Not bad. Not great, but not bad.

So there was a time I would have said yes, starting out in Penticton was the worst decision I could have made. I would have said it around the time I was digging through a mountain of receipts on that card table set up in the middle of the dance floor. I would definitely have said it moments before Les Edgelow walked through the door that afternoon. I'd fantasize about Prince George. I'd wonder, if we had opened there instead, would things have been better, different, easier? But I don't live by ifs: if a cow had nuts, it'd be a bull. Mostly, if we hadn't made the decision to open up in Penticton, I would never have met George.

Show How Helping You Will Benefit Them

George had straightened up our books, but there was the lingering issue of the 10% royalty to Gus. It was too high. But since Gus had no other franchisees, only corporate stores that didn't pay him a portion of their sales, it was hard to make the case that our fee was indeed too high. He'd only need to look at our books, though, to see that, at that rate, we'd never clear enough profit to grow. Since I didn't speak "accounting," I asked George to make a road trip with me to Edmonton, to talk Gus down from 10% to 7%.

"I think it's time you met Gus," I told him.

By then, Gus had several stores running in Edmonton, and he was opening franchises in Winnipeg and Calgary.

Gus had also partnered with a man named Ian Barrigan, an Edmonton banker who later became Wayne Gretzky's financial advisor. We made plans to meet them both, to see if we could negotiate a more reasonable franchise fee. But George didn't drive with me to Edmonton for free. He charged me a daily per diem for any days that fell between Monday and Friday. I persuaded him to leave with me on a Sunday to save a buck.

It's hard to argue with numbers, I've discovered. When your situation is spelled out in black and white, you can talk until the cows come home, but the facts are still the facts: we were about to stagnate at that 10% rate. We explained to Gus that it would be better to get 7% from several healthy restaurants than 10% from one struggling store.

Gus understood those numbers. And he was a reasonable man. He realized that we had to make money or the whole enterprise would collapse. But here's the thing: in order to pay Gus the back fees we owed him (about $4,000), we had to borrow more money . . . from Gus. And he happily lent it—on one condition. We couldn't tell his brothers, who were stricter than he was. Boston Pizza was a family-owned business and there was always a little drama behind the scenes, always some pushing and pulling. The less the brothers knew about our new deal, the better, and not just for us but also for Gus.

Mostly Gus lent us the money because he wanted us to succeed. He also dialed the franchise fee back from 10% to 7% for the following year, and for every one of our franchises thereafter, without which we would not have grown so quickly. (The rate of 7% is what we charge today.) Gus didn't like many lawyers or accountants, but he liked George; he trusted him and his numbers.

I felt a little triumphant on the ride back, but the feeling didn't last. Just outside Revelstoke, the car up and died. George and I got out and walked into the night. It must have been one or two o'clock in the morning, and so dark the air almost felt inky on my skin. I was calculating the cost of towing and fixing the car, plus the added day George would charge me for his services, all the while thinking, *The universe gives with one hand and takes with the other.* Luckily, a car pulled over to help. Luckier still, the driver was heading straight through to Penticton. I stayed behind in Revelstoke to deal with the car in the morning but sent George home so he wouldn't charge me for an extra day. Those few hours with George before the car broke down solidified something for me: my understanding of what a true partnership could offer.

A friend of mine owned a flying school. Every weekend he'd take Don and me for piloting lessons, eventually handing us a plane, which we'd use to scope out new locations for Boston Pizzas. The first place we flew to was my old RCMP stomping grounds. Prince George was by now a small city, and it was booming. We found an excellent location near a new hotel, and later Don returned to oversee construction. I followed a few months later to help open the restaurant. During a fishing trip, we found the third location, in Prince Rupert. I spotted a for-rent sign in what looked like another perfect location in town, near hotels, and with ample parking. I called the number on the sign. A Ray McCarthy answered. He was in Vancouver, about to board a plane to Whitehorse. I persuaded him to meet me halfway, in Prince George, to talk about leasing terms. I took the midnight bus and Ray booked a stopover. We met at the bar in the Inn of the North, and we wrote up the leasing terms for the building in Prince Rupert on the back of a coaster. By November 1970, we had our third location, where we also operated a busy nightclub in the basement.

By this time, Cheryl was starting school and Brad was a toddler, and my life was heading into high gear. I think about how I missed Cheryl's birth because I was on assignment with the RCMP. I missed Brad's too because of work, which was doubly bad because he was born on my wife's birthday. I have no excuses, no apologies, it's just the way it was.

In a five-year span, we opened a total of four franchises: Penticton, Prince George, Prince Rupert and Kamloops. We were opening them even before paying off our creditors. We were learning that healthy debt isn't always a bad thing: needing to pay what we owed was an incentive to keep growing the chain. We also had our eye on Kelowna and Vernon. By the mid-1970s, George was working for us pretty much full time. Everything he suggested we do, we did. He told us we needed to hire a full-time book-keeper, so we did, a woman named Gwen Philpott. He advised us to amalgamate our bank accounts, so we did. He told us we needed to raise the price of our pizzas, so we . . . talked about it. He suggested upping food prices a dollar across the board, which was a huge deal and the only idea of his at which we hesitated. When we did raise the prices, I thought there'd be a backlash, but the only person who complained was the owner of a motel who had given our old menu to a guest, who was angry at the price change when he got his bill.

Whether you should take the leap from salaried worker to entrepreneur is a big decision to make. But it's not the riskiest. You're close enough to your old job and your old life that folding up and retreating when you find out a year or two in that working for yourself is not for you isn't really such a big defeat. I wish more people would do that instead of holding on to a dying venture or stubbornly refusing to believe that they're not entrepreneur material to begin with. Even when I had my doubts during that first Penticton winter, even when the very survival of Boston Pizza was in question, I still believed that I was meant to be an entrepreneur. I was willing to do whatever it took to make the restaurant work before I would go back to collecting a paycheque. I had crossed the line. I was an entrepreneur. There was no going backwards.

Pay Good People Great Money

In 1973, it became apparent to me that we needed George full time, on payroll. He was a rising star at Peat Marwick; his was a stable, secure job. But he was also intimate with our bottom line. There was money to be made in the pizza business, and he knew it. And he also knew we had a sound business model because, well, he helped to create the damn thing. I hoped that by offering him a higher salary than even Don and I were earning, he'd be game. You have to do that for good people: you have to pay them more than yourself sometimes. If they're worth it, it's a decision you'll never regret. Don hesitated at first because he knew that George and I got on like a house on fire. I could bounce ideas off George and, instead of shutting me down, he would try to figure out how to make them work. I would give him a problem and he could find a great solution. He really listened to my point of view. Don had good reason to feel threatened.

Don eventually agreed to hire George as our accountant and chief financial officer. And he was fine with a lot of his ideas too. But when I suggested a year later that we give George shares and make him a minority partner, the sauce really hit the fan. Don didn't see the point in giving up any equity. He couldn't see value in George's contribution, and I began to see less and less value in Don's.

I didn't back down on my proposal. I insisted that we each give up 10%, making George a 20% partner. That's when the cracks in my partnership with Don began to show, and I realized I was about to make yet another difficult but necessary decision. I was about take on a new 50-50 partner, but not before cutting the old one loose.

Checklist for Making Decisions about Money

Asking for money is one of the hardest things entrepreneurs do. That's why I think it makes for compelling TV. On *Dragons' Den*, when the financial stakes are high and a pitcher gets a deal, it's like watching a focused golfer finally land a hole-in-one. I see a little bit of myself in almost every entrepreneur who comes down those stairs. The mere act of asking for money or financial backing brings out a person's true nature. Here are a few things to keep in mind next time you go looking, hat-in-hand, for an investment, whether to a bank, a parent, a Dragon, or a potential partner:

1. Finances Are a Face-to-Face Deal. I list this point first because it should be the first rule of thumb. I met with George face to face with my financial problems, and we met with our creditors face to face with our financial solution. I've always asked for money from key investors in person, including my dad. Even though I could have easily made a phone call to Manitoba, instead I hitched a ride across three provinces to talk to my dad in person, after which I met with Mr. Dumpleton face to face. Although I believe money decisions should never be made emotionally, they should never be made remotely either. Even in our era of instant this, and technological that, I say get on a plane, get in your car and get off your butt when it comes to matters of money.

2. When in Doubt (and Debt), Choose Transparency. This was the most important lesson we learned after our first Penticton winter, and I've heeded it ever since. Don't keep people in the dark about money, especially if you owe them. Be transparent about how you plan to pay the money back. It's rarely the money itself, but rather the lack of information, that causes anxiety and bad blood. Remember, it's not your money, it's theirs. Show them where it's currently being used, and how you plan to free it up and give it back. Debt collectors will tell you that they'd much prefer an open dialogue with the debtor than evasiveness. If you can't pay it all back at once, talk about what you *can* pay back. Try to come to an equitable agreement on a schedule. Nine times out of 10, information will alleviate pretty much all the aggravation.

3. Readjust, Don't Renege. I go back to my dad's advice: Don't just hire an accountant, listen to them. George didn't just spot our financing problems, he helped us adjust our schedule of payments, better balancing our cash flow. He created a sound financial structure. Before that, I thought our only options were liens on our establishment, defaulting on payments and maybe even bankruptcy. I didn't know we could restructure the way we did business. A good accountant will walk you through the options.

4. Financial Uncertainty Breeds Ingenuity. I know more than anyone that awful pit-of-the-stomach feeling that financial insecurity can create. You don't even want to get out of bed in the morning when you have big debt hanging over your business. After I got over the initial fear and started to seek help, that period of uncertainty ended up being a boon. We were able to see what really worked and what didn't, and we made recipe and menu adjustments that helped increase our margins. We also raised our prices. People want quality and value, and they're willing to pay a little more for it.

5. Asking for Money Is a Skill—Get Good at It. You see it on *Dragons' Den*. You can spot the winners, the ones who have pitching down to a science, who make me lean forward so I can carefully listen to the story of their business and why I should invest my money in it. I have a hard time hiding enthusiasm for a great idea, especially when being pitched to in a compelling way. A pitcher's sound valuation is the sign that I can invest with confidence. They understand what they have, what they need and how I can help.

5

WHO WILL JOIN ME?

Picking the Right Partners,
Cutting the Wrong Ones Loose

*"Surround yourself with partners
who are better than you are."*
—David Ogilvy

Shared Principles Equals Strong Partnerships

I am lucky to have been raised by happy people. My parents were both themselves happy, and you could tell that they got a real kick out of being together, which made them great to be around. They were opposites in a lot of ways. My dad was shy, somewhat taciturn. My mom loved playing cards and socializing. But they had the same simple goals: raising a family, being kind to each other and contributing to the community. And they were profoundly loyal partners.

When I started to make a little money at Boston Pizza, I went home to Virden for a visit. Before heading to my folks' house, I made a quick stop at Marshall's Hardware. I wanted to buy them something special, something they wouldn't think to buy for themselves. Something that would show them I'd finally made it. My parents had a nightly ritual after dinner: my mom washed the dishes, and my dad stood next to her, drying and putting them away. If you wanted to keep talking to them, you had to go into the kitchen and chat with them at the sink, their backs turned to you. So I thought it would be great to buy them a dishwasher—that way we could sit and chat while the after-dinner chores were taken care of.

I ordered the appliance and paid to have it delivered and installed the day I arrived. When my dad came home from work, he took one look at it in the kitchen, thanked me and then told me to rip it out and take it back where I had bought it.

"Why, Dad? You're both getting on in years. And you entertain a lot," I said. "A dishwasher will make your life a lot easier."

"I don't want my life to get easier. I like it just the way it is. I want to keep standing next to your beautiful mother every night," he said. He was more attached to that small, intimate ritual than he was attracted to the convenience of a dishwasher. He was that kind of man. With my parents, I never got the sense that there was a chink in their armour that I could penetrate. They were a solid, united front. He worked; she stayed at home with the kids. There was no swearing in the house, and we were taught to respect our elders. They had a great partnership because it was built on a bedrock of shared principles and goals, enhanced by different abilities.

That was the problem with me and Don: we didn't have the same goals. He didn't want to grow the business as big as I did, or as fast as I thought we could. And because both of us were outgoing and gregarious, our strengths overlapped. Ours was not a broad partnership covering all the bases. My developing a good rapport with George only highlighted how bad things had begun to get between Don and me. Communication had begun to break down. He had started to leave notes on my desk if he had anything to say to me—not a good sign. But Boston Pizza was growing so fast I didn't have time to worry over that relationship, or fix it. Not then, anyway.

By 1978, Gus Agioritis had 42 Boston Pizza outlets up and running. Some were franchises like the 16 stores Don, George and I operated in the BC Interior, others were corporate stores he and his brothers ran. But things with the brothers had also begun to come apart, with one of Gus's younger brothers opening his own pizza chain, called Trifon's, in Saskatchewan. Gus was beginning to branch out into the commercial real estate business too, and since he was the last of the brothers to get married, he had young children at home just as he was inching towards middle age. So, after 14 years in the business, Gus came to the conclusion that he wanted out. It was time to sell Boston Pizza. He approached one of his franchisees (and best friends) in Edmonton, a guy named Ron Coyle who owned four successful franchises in the city. With financial backing from Jim and Mac Millar, Ron bought the company and Gus left the restaurant business. He was barely 40. But it wasn't time for him to retire. Gus went on to invest in oil and gas, and he owned and managed a string of apartment buildings—a great immigrant success story.

I owe a lot to Gus Agioritis. A lot of us do. He changed the landscape of casual dining in Canada. He took risks on people who had no restaurant experience because in his gut he knew they had what it took to pull it off. Think about owning a successful business, branching out and then letting someone take your concept to another province, someone whose only real skill is enthusiasm. That's what Gus did for me. And he was rarely wrong about people when he listened to his gut. He taught me that too.

Now Boston Pizza had a new boss and would enter a new era. Ron Coyle was to be our franchisor now, and the 7% fee from our stores would go to him. The first thing Ron did as the new owner was to change the name of the company to Boston Pizza International. The "international" signalled Ron's intentions and his scope. He wanted Boston Pizza to cover Canada and eventually other parts of the world. With Ron came more structure, more professionalism and more uniformity. Far from resisting this, Don, George and I embraced the new discipline. I had a feeling I was going to like our new franchisor, and I was right. Ron and I became fast friends, and he supported our rapid growth.

Not long after Ron took over the company, he lost his own business partner, Gordon Hammond, to cancer. It was devastating for Ron because, like me, he operated best in a vital partnership. He soon turned to George and me for help. He offered us Gord's shares, though not all of them, only about 15% of the company. But he asked us to move back to Edmonton to help him run the company, while still keeping our homes and franchises in BC. Don Spence wasn't part of this partnership—he stayed behind to run our BC franchises. But he had already begun to make himself scarce. It didn't matter; the part-time partnership experiment proved to be short-lived.

One big problem surfaced almost immediately. Our decision-making styles were different—very different. Ron deliberated over every move. He'd choose a path, and then he'd second-guess himself. And sometimes he'd make a decision, then veto parts of it, rendering the whole thing pretty useless. Right away, George and I knew that Ron wasn't going to bend to our style of decision making, which was built on mutual trust. When George and I agreed on a decision, we immediately put it into action. Regardless of who came up with the solution, we were both responsible for the outcome, good or bad. There was never blame if it steered us in the wrong direction, and neither of us took credit if it landed us someplace better. We knew each other in a way that would take Ron a long time to catch up. Besides, it was pretty clear Ron would always think of himself as the majority partner who held the veto, who could neuter a crucial decision regardless of whether George and I were sure it was the right one. That alone was a powder keg of potential problems. And before there was a blowout, before we took a fatal turn, we ended the temporary partnership and left for BC with our business still intact, and our relationship with Ron still in a good place. Stopping that partnership in its tracks was a very smart decision—and it laid the groundwork for the big changes ahead.

The time with Ron did whet our entrepreneurial appetites. George and I realized we wanted to helm something that was our own. We looked into opening other kinds of franchises, and we started meeting with developers to branch out into commercial real estate. In 1980, we partnered with my cousin Bob Gardner and started a company called Mighty Peace Oil Services Ltd., which rented heavy equipment to oil companies in northern Alberta. It was based in Fort St. John, so we flew back and forth quite a bit as we expanded into chemicals and trucking. The company did so well, Bob eventually bought us out, and the company's still operating today.

This was a time I was on the road for months at a stretch, moving non-stop. To say I worked 24 hours a day is not an exaggeration. I slept in planes and cars, and some mornings it would take a second or two for me to remember where I was and what town I had woken up in. But I was having the time of my life, existing on pure adrenaline. It's the fatal flaw of every driven entrepreneur, putting everything second to the business—family, friends and, in my case, my health.

Know Who Has Your Back

At first, I thought the hacking cough was just part of a lingering cold. But when I woke one morning too weak to put on my socks, I knew something was really wrong. I had double pneumonia and was so sick that, for the first time in my life, I had to have my doctor make a house call. He ordered bed rest for a month, which seemed inconceivable to me, until I realized that I couldn't even lift my head off my pillow to complain. I had run myself down to the ground. It was so bad that Don initiated discussions with George about what to do in the event of my death. In fact, he went so far as to suggest that they buy me out then and there because, even if I recovered, I might never be the same. That told me two things: I was quite sick, and my partnership with Don was in deep trouble.

George wouldn't hear of it.

That signalled the end of my relationship with Don. There I was, sweating it out in bed, and instead of bringing me soup, Don was considering staging a coup.

Luckily, I recovered fully. Elaine and I were living in Tsawwassen, a city in BC's Lower Mainland, then. This was our first real house, the first one we bought, and I couldn't have been prouder of it—or more satisfied. After I was back on my feet, I flew my parents in for a weekend visit. I wanted them to see how their son had finally made it. We were growing and expanding, and I was living in a massive two-storey house on a beautiful street with a big backyard, cathedral ceilings and a built-in pool. It had cost just over $100,000, a fortune at the time. (That same house is probably worth more than a million dollars today.) I also invited the neighbours and their kids over for a meet-and-greet. A dentist lived next to us on one side, a pilot on the other.

After dinner, as the kids were splashing around in the pool

and Elaine opened another bottle of wine, the pilot asked me, seemingly out of nowhere, if I was going to renegotiate my mortgage. Rates were as high as 15% at the time, and I had recently closed at 9.5%, which was considered a bargain.

"No, I got a good rate. I'm going to leave it alone," I said, trying to change the subject. The "M" word had caused the ember of my dad's cigar to redden in the dark.

In the late 1970s, inflation and interest rates were the main topic of conversation at dinner tables across the country. If you had a mortgage, you were bleeding money to the bank. I knew what my dad was thinking: *My son has a mortgage. I haven't taught him anything.* The pilot went on and on about his mortgage for another painful 20 minutes. The whole time my dad just listened.

Later, after seeing the final guests out, I headed back to the patio, where my dad's cigar had shrunk to an angry stump and the inevitable lecture awaited me.

"I'm proud of you, Jim," he said. *Here it comes,* I thought. "This is a nice big house. You got some nice cars parked outside too. But make no mistake, if you have a mortgage, if you've financed those cars, you don't own any of it."

Upon hearing this, my mother and Elaine, who had just come out with after-dinner coffees, made U-turns and headed back inside.

I felt defensive. "Yeah, I own it, Dad. I'm paying for it all."

"No, you don't, Jim, the bank owns all of this."

I didn't reply. I was in my 30s and still couldn't shake off the need for my father's approval.

"Jim, do you know that in the 1930s, if you couldn't make

a payment, the bank took your house and put you out on the street? What if the rates went up to 20%? Could you afford the payments then?"

"I could. Besides, they won't go up that high."

They could, and they did.

To the day he died, my dad was a cash-only kind of guy. As a child of the Great Depression, he never shook off his mortal fear of debt. And banks to him were not benevolent entities out to give someone a hand. They kept people shackled. There is a lot of wisdom in his way of thinking. But there's also a lot of fear. In business and life, I've tried to find a balance between risk and growth. To grow, I needed to borrow money. To secure those loans, I had to take on some risk. Luckily for me, it paid off. Even with my home, even with those high interest rates, I could always afford my mortgage payments. And strategic debt helped Boston Pizza grow. Even as we were paying off debt from opening one Boston Pizza, we were securing financing to open the next one, and the next one and the next one.

My dad dropped the subject after we agreed to disagree.

Those late nights by the pool, I thought we'd live in Tsawwassen forever. I remember having a feeling that we had it all—the house, two kids, a growing company. But the more successful my businesses became, the more my marriage came apart at the seams. The constant travel, the long days and the late nights had finally taken their toll on us.

I get asked this a lot from up-and-coming entrepreneurs: How do you find that balance between work and family when you're building a new business? I just don't think you do. Balance is a myth. For many entrepreneurs, work comes first—it has to—and if you're lucky, your marriage will survive those early tumultuous years when you're building your business. If there is a formula, or a better way to balance it all out, I don't know it. Me, I couldn't pull it off. That said, Elaine's and my separation and divorce was as amicable as they get. To this day, she remains a good friend and has always been a great mother. My daughter, Cheryl, went to law school and is now the executive director of the Boston Pizza Foundation. Brad played professional hockey before joining the NHL, becoming the assistant general manager of the Phoenix Coyotes. I'm proud of both of them, but I give Elaine full credit for raising our children. And I'm grateful to her.

Sometimes Opportunity Doesn't Knock, It Barges In

My marriage wasn't the only casualty. My partnership with Don had suffered. Firing someone is difficult enough, ending a partnership is wrenching. And ours was not a happy parting. When I broke the news to Don that I no longer wanted to be in business with him, he wasn't surprised, but he was angry. Naturally, lawyers were involved, with negotiations as intense as any divorce. Don didn't want to meet face to face. We came to a buyout price we all agreed on, but when it came time to sign our dissolution papers, Don wanted it to take place in different rooms, with lawyers running back and forth down the hall. When it was all done, he asked me to stay in the building until he left. I haven't seen him since.

This was the early 1980s, a time of major growth for Boston Pizza, but in BC, we were beginning to feel hemmed in and underutilized. Don't get me wrong, Ron Coyle was a visionary who introduced formal franchisee meetings and national conventions, and he wrote the first operations manuals for the whole chain. These were necessary and important policies. Ron also updated the Boston Pizza look, brushing off the last vestiges of the Greek motif that had followed us around for ages. Under his leadership, Boston Pizza ruled the casual dining market in western Canada. And even though our brief partnership didn't pan out, we loved the guy.

But it was George and I who were increasingly coming up with new innovations, including co-op advertising, where franchisees paid a set amount for a consistent campaign that would work for all restaurants across provinces. We also instituted annual meetings, and we were known for our strong focus on service. Also, all our restaurants offered delivery, whereas those in Alberta didn't. So we felt we needed to be able to make more decisions about the direction of the company. We had planned to discuss this with Ron the day we picked him up from the airport in Vancouver. He was flying in from Boston Pizza headquarters, which then was still in Edmonton. He had some business to conduct with us, his biggest franchisees. But George and I were also Ron's friends, and we had a sense that this visit was going to be more social than business, as he was going through a tough divorce, due in part to his constant travelling. Having had some experience with this,

I was looking forward to a long dinner with drinks and commiserating.

But that's not what happened. At the corner of 41st and Granville, the car idling at a red light, Ron turned to me and said, "Have you guys ever thought about buying the whole company? Running the whole damn thing yourselves? I think I'm done."

The timing could not have been better. In fact, George and I had already discussed how, if we couldn't expand, if we couldn't make more decisions about the direction in which we wanted to go, we were either going to get out of Boston Pizza altogether or start our own franchise. I never thought what Ron was now suggesting could be possible, and I was speechless.

"What do you say, guys? You want to buy the company?"

"Yes. We do. What's the price?"

"Four million."

When we eventually got out of the car, George turned to me and whispered, "Jim! Where do you think we're going to get that kind of money?"

"Well, he didn't ask us that, George. He just asked us if we want to buy the company. We do, don't we?"

"Yeah, but . . . the money?"

"We'll figure that out later."

Why did Ron want to sell? Because he was a clever businessman. He knew the company had to grow, big and fast, and now was the time. But he also knew the best thing he could do was step aside. He had the humility to know he wasn't up for the next phase, and he had the smarts to know that we were.

Always Leave Something on the Table

The big question was where to get that kind of money. Although we couldn't ignore that uncertainty, we did, on the other hand, have two very real certainties. One: Going forward, it was just going to be George and me. And two: We'd split everything down the middle 50-50. You could argue that I was in a position, having co-founded the first Boston Pizza franchise, to offer George a less equitable split, maybe 30% or even 40%, which would have generously doubled his stake. But that idea never crossed my mind. Partnering for less than half would have seemed an insult. I wanted George to have skin in the game beyond his skills and his personality. He was already doing an incredible job as a minority partner. I figured the more he benefited from the health and growth of the company, the better we'd all do. That was the best investment I've ever made. And I give my dad the credit, for teaching me to be generous at the right times, to the right people.

I remember once bragging to my dad about a sweetheart land deal where I bought a nice piece of property that I sold for quadruple the price soon after. "And I squeezed every single nickel out of that buyer," I added, expecting a pat on the back from my dad. I thought he'd marvel at my wheeling and dealing. Instead he looked at me and said, "That doesn't sound like a good deal to me at all, Jim."

"What do you mean? I sold the land for four times what I paid for it. I made a small fortune."

"Jim, a good deal is when you leave a little something on the table."

He meant that I was in a position to be generous, to have taken a little less, given a bit more of a bargain to the buyer. Why? In case I ever had to do business with him again. Business is a small world. According to my dad, now I'd be forever known as the guy who squeezed him for a nickel.

"People know when they overpay," he said, "and that feeling lingers long after the lawyers go home."

That was the last time I ever did that kind of deal, let alone bragged about it to my dad. And that was also the last time I ever got to do business with that buyer. I had learned my lesson. I wouldn't be less than generous with George.

What was it about George and me that clicked? Both of us came from great organizations—George from the accounting firm Peat Marwick, which eventually became KPMG, and I from the RCMP. So we cut our teeth in organizations where to rise through the ranks forced you to grow a thicker skin and gain some ingenuity. And we had respect for structure and discipline. When something worked, we instituted it. We also believed in group conscience—looking to what's best for the company rather than for any one individual. These are not small things. Coming from companies with terrific traditions meant we were always sensitive to building our own traditions, right from the get-go. We bonded over a shared vision of the company. I would have an idea, and he would lay out the financial groundwork. He could see the strengths and weaknesses and suggest alternative routes to success. There was no such thing as a stupid idea or an impossible vision with George, and I began to feel even more comfortable in my entrepreneurial skin because I finally had a partner whom I trusted completely.

Seek Backing from People Like You, Not Just People You Like

Back to the $4 million: to put it bluntly, we didn't have it. Not even a little of it. That meant new partners, the rich kind, the kind who'd be willing to part with cash for a hefty chunk of the business, and who'd be happy to let us run the place ourselves. No small order.

Problem was, I wasn't a member of the chamber of commerce. Back then, I didn't spend a lot of time networking and glad-handing with other local business people, mostly because I was too damn busy actually working.

George and I sat down and made a list of people we knew who had *that kind of money* and an itch to invest in a couple of guys with a very big dream. We had eventually talked Ron Coyle down from $4 million to $3.5 million— better, but it was still an inconceivable amount.

High on my list was a local entrepreneur named Dave Gillespie, whose son, Mark, I coached in hockey. Dave and I became good friends, and George and I often had lunch at the Richmond Inn, which Dave co-owned with another wealthy man named Bud Grant. Dave, like George, was an accountant, so in many ways Bud and Dave's partnership mirrored the dynamic of my partnership with George, with Bud being the dreamer and Dave being the pragmatic money guy. I picked up the phone and did something many would-be entrepreneurs find very difficult: I called Dave to ask him for money. After some small talk about hockey, I came right out with it.

"Dave, George and I have a once-in-a-lifetime opportunity to buy Boston Pizza—the whole company. Ron Coyle's selling, and we think it's a hell of a deal, but we're looking for money and we need a partner. Wonder if it's something you'd be interested in."

"How much are you talking about?"

"About $3.8 million." (We tacked on $300,000 extra to go towards setting up a new office and to do some hiring.) I waited for him to make an excuse and get off the phone. Instead, Dave told us to come right over to meet with his partner, Bud Grant. I hung up and looked at George.

"They want a meeting."

"When?"

"Today."

George spent the rest of the morning putting together a rough five-year business plan. It laid out a trajectory of growth Boston Pizza could undergo with our leadership and their money, and a confident payment plan that clearly indicated that this was a terrific investment opportunity for all involved.

Arriving at Dave's office, we all shook hands. George handed out copies of his solidly constructed plan. Dave glanced at the document and flung it aside. Then he said three simple words: "Let's do it."

They agreed to give us $1.5 million, and an additional $300,000 to set up headquarters and pay some bills. Ron Coyle, who knew Bud and Dave well, agreed to finance the remaining $2 million—with 10% interest—over a five-year period. So without putting down any of our own money (well, we paid a nominal fee for our shares), George and I owned 50% of Boston Pizza International, Bud and Dave the other half. They got compensated for their money with interest payments, we got compensated with our pay-cheques. Everyone felt it was a good deal. Actually, George and I thought it was a great one.

We were financed properly for the first time in our business lives. The possibilities were endless. Dave and Bud were the perfect partners. As long as the cheques rolled in and there were lineups at the restaurants, they were happy. But I think what made them happiest was that we kept them informed, maybe even overly informed, if that's possible. They received monthly financial statements from us, detailing the cash flow of the entire business. In fact, we gave them information before they asked for it, some they probably didn't need. What I've come to realize after my experience with Don was that a partner's concerns about a problem are often bigger than the actual problem. That's why there is no such thing as too much information. Information combats fear and doubt. It builds trust. So we communicated everything to Dave and Bud. We treated them as partners, not just financers. This allowed them to relax and to trust us.

Once, when our cash flow was tight, I called up Dave and asked him to hold off processing one of the postdated cheques for a couple of weeks.

"Sure, no problem," Dave said. He didn't even need

to know what the problem was. Soon, our cash flow improved and I gave Dave the go-ahead to cash the cheque. But a while later, our accountant noticed something strange. Dave hadn't cashed *any* of our cheques for months, not since the day we had asked him for that delay. I called him up.

"Dave, what's going on? You're not cashing our cheques."

"Oh, jeez. I totally forgot to call up my guy and tell him to start putting them through again," he said. "I'll do it right now."

This told me that Dave and Bud enjoyed a certain level of comfort with us; they knew our cheques would clear, so there was no sense of urgency.

So why did Dave and Bud not hesitate to partner with us? A lot of it, I think, had to do with my being a hockey coach and an active member of the community. That counted for a lot in business—still does. Dave saw that I was not only passionate, committed and accountable, but that I was a team player. I didn't learn that in business. I didn't learn that in school. I learned it by playing team sports.

I played a lot of hockey growing up. I played for the sheer love of the game and the camaraderie. (Okay, and the girls.) To this day, I can tell by his or her personality if a person was a team-sport player or a solo competitor. (I can also spot a goalie—a combination of both.) Think of the personality differences between Sidney Crosby and Tiger Woods. When you're part of a team, your worst character traits are often softened by your teammates because their strengths are often in areas where you're weakest.

The other thing about team sports is you can't get away with arrogance for too long. Your teammates will have at you. You also can't take all the credit. You can't hog the puck or ball. You can't slack off. You can't criticize, blame or isolate for long when you're part of a bustling movement with the same goal. People who are a part of an active healthy team don't have a lot of blunt edges to their characters.

On the other hand, to be a great golfer, you have to be able to go it alone, to be deeply internal, to find strength from inside yourself and keep your own counsel. That's probably the reason the game didn't intrigue me until my late 40s, when I started to develop more maturity and get comfortable in my own skin. When you play golf, all eyes are on you all the time, and it's up to you and you alone. Always. That has a harsh effect on a person's character. I'm not saying all golfers are a little "off." I'm saying if you live by principles that put *you* before anything and everyone else, *you* have to work extra hard to combat the kind of character defects that can set in and derail you. These two sports, hockey and golf, breed very different kinds of athletes. And players from each sport follow a very different set of principles. For my money, pro hockey players are a lot more fun to be around than pro golfers. I'm generalizing when I say this, of course, but the hockey players are often enthusiastic, spirited and welcoming types, whereas the golfers tend to be more solitary, a bit standoffish. They're just different breeds of athletes. Don't get me wrong, I love golf, but I have always preferred playing on a team, and with Bud, Dave and George, I felt we had a winning one.

One of the smart things we did was to ask for money from people like us, people who'd built something similar because others believed in *their* dream. Their investments meant that George and I didn't have to go to a faceless bank and pay exorbitant interest rates to realize our dream. Bud backed Dave in the hotel business, and Dave proved to Bud he was a good bet. They backed us, they said, not because they wanted to be in the pizza business but because they wanted to be in business with us. When people give you that kind of confidence, it adds incredible momentum to the endeavour. It makes you that much more determined to succeed.

Splitting Focus Stunts Growth

On February 1, 1983, papers were signed officially making us the owners of Boston Pizza. It was time to take stock, to decide what kind of company we wanted to helm. We looked around at other successful franchises, in particular McDonald's and Kentucky Fried Chicken. Both companies were and are a combination of corporate stores and franchises. Boston Pizza was too, at the time. George and I soon realized we had to decide exactly what kind of business we were in and what kind of company we wanted to build. True, we had just bought a restaurant chain, but it was clear to both of us that to grow, we had to get out of the restaurant business.

When Ron sold the company to us, there were 38 stores, a healthy blend of corporate and franchises. We often made more money from our corporate stores than we did from franchisees. A successful store generates about a 20%

profit. If you own the store, that's your money. If you are the franchisor, you're getting only 7% of the food sales, but you're not spending valuable time actually operating the store. Someone else is doing that. Franchises and corporate stores are two different businesses. To do both, you have to wear two different hats, and that can hamper your business's development.

To become the best-franchised restaurant in the world, we realized that we had to do one thing and one thing well. We had to become franchisors. That's all. In a year, we sold all the corporate stores. It wasn't difficult to do. In most cases, we had operating partners already running the stores. We just had to negotiate a price with them or help them get financing to buy us out fully. Boston Pizzas were money makers, and everyone who knew anything about restaurant franchising was eager to buy his or her own.

After that, we hired a guy named Bruce Fox to head operations and sent him on the road to do an inventory of all the stores. Every one of them. We called it "solidifying the base," which meant we had to ensure that each of our current stores was sound and profitable before we opened another one. George and I got on planes to meet franchisees, people we didn't know, people who had worked under Ron Coyle, or Gus before him. At the time of our takeover there was one store under construction in Edmonton. The franchisee, Gary Simmons, was close friends with Ron. After Ron sold the company to us, Gary called to say he had changed his mind. He wanted his franchise fee back. He no longer wanted to become a franchisee under our leadership.

We flew out there to meet him. We knew the only problem was that he didn't know us well. He had a personal relationship with Ron, not us. Today, he's still one of our best franchisees. He just needed to meet us, to hear what our vision was and how, under us, Boston Pizza would continue to thrive and grow.

I also remember coming down hard on another franchisee who wanted to copy a rival's two-for-one pizza deal in his delivery service. He argued that it would be a big enough seller to make up for some lost restaurant revenue. Maybe so, but I convinced him he'd be better off improving his in-house dining experience than encouraging cheaper home-delivery prices. Soon after improving ambience, service and staff morale, as well as making his franchise more kid-friendly, sales in the dining room took off. He realized that he didn't need to react by discounting the hell out of his product in order to improve his business.

The problem with wanting to rush in and compete with a two-for-one delivery deal is that it was a reaction to a market downtrend, not a decision to correct it. Rather than mimicking what your competition is doing, it's better to focus on what you do better, and then decide to spend your energy and money there. Reacting to something rather than deliberating over a strategy is a mistake many businesses make. When you react, you're correcting something that has just happened, and often doing it without thinking.

Ron didn't have the stomach to keep franchisees in line. That's partly because he was a franchisee himself—a fundamental problem. It's hard to be detached and objective.

It's hard to crack down on people doing something you yourself have done or want to do to cut corners. That's why it was key for George and me to get out of the business of running the corporate stores ourselves. When we took over the company, we began by closing four weak stores, one in Calgary, one in Abbotsford, one in Victoria and another in Hinton, Alberta. Then we moved corporate head offices from Edmonton to Richmond, BC, where we also kept one corporate store where we would test recipes and train staff. As well, we fine-tuned our manuals, standardized more recipes and hired more support staff to handle purchasing, design and marketing. We were now solely in the business of serving our franchisees. That decision meant that we were no longer two things at once, which allowed us to concentrate on the next phase: growing and expanding the company.

Checklist for Making Decisions about Partnerships

For me, partnerships are a winning formula. I can't stress this enough. There are plenty of successful companies helmed by lone-wolf types. But I believe the longevity of our company and its steady growth can be attributed to the fact that there have always been two of us at the helm, spelling each other off, giving the other a break. Teamwork has help us build stamina because neither one of us had to carry the whole thing on our shoulders. Here are a few pointers to keep in mind when you're considering hiring or partnering with someone:

1. Roots of Good Partnerships Start at Home. I learned from my parents that the essence of any good partnership is communication. Without that you've got nothing. However, even if you didn't grow up in an ideal environment, consider that you have another advantage: you know what *doesn't* work, and the kind of relationships you *don't* want. That is, dysfunction too can teach you something valuable. Figure out what that is for you. There's also no excuse these days for poor communication. And although email and texting have become indispensable—I've come to love keeping in touch with people via Twitter—important matters are a face-to-face deal.

When we designed the head offices in Richmond from scratch, we made our individual offices adjoining, with a meeting room in the middle and a lot of glass so we could always see where the other was at. Seeing George around was reassuring for me. It may seem a little odd, but when we realized our partnership worked, we built our company on notions and traditions that supported that partnership. Besides sharing offices, we ate lunch together every single day. (This was before I moved to Toronto and then Dallas, Texas. Now we schedule regular conferences calls and meet-ups, which have become even more important as Boston Pizza continues to expand globally.) But we talk, face to face. We hash things out in person. Over the years, George and I have become like one of those happily long-married couples who can finish each other's sentences, who knows what the other is thinking. A healthy partnership brings a stability to the company.

2. Partnerships Must Change—Together. I know few people whose initial business partnerships weathered the early storms. (Let alone first marriages, but that's a different book.) Don Spence and I didn't make it. We both had a lot of enthusiasm starting out. But although enthusiasm is important when you make the decision to embark on a new venture, it doesn't sustain healthy relationships. Loyalty does. When I entered the next stage of my entrepreneurial development, I was looking for loyalty, for a partner I could count on in times of trouble and change. Nine times out of 10, you're not firing people or ending partnerships because of lack of skill. It's almost always about character and personality. Talent is important, experience indispensable, but if someone doesn't fit into the culture of the company, none of that will matter.

3. You Are the Company. When I was a franchisee, I was a wilder guy, whipping around the country and having a lot of fun. If we were in a town with another Boston Pizza, we always had a few drinks with the local franchisee. We were in the same boat and shared stories of our frustrations and successes over several beers. I had a lot of energy, and I always brought it with me wherever I went. When George and I bought the company, we became the bosses, the standard setters, the franchisors. That meant I had to change, tone things down and set an example. We were the decision makers now. We were also sensitive to the fact that we each represented our company, and once we bought it, we began to conduct ourselves accordingly at work and with franchisees.

4. Know Your Local Luminaries. Potential partners and investors are often right underneath your nose. (Remember, I coached Dave Gillespie's son in hockey.) They live in your community, they work near you and they probably go to your gym. Like I said, I was never much of a chamber of commerce type, but I've since come to learn the value of being a member of something, even if it's just my local golf club, Kiwanis or gym. Read your community newspapers and use social media to make these kinds of contacts. One of the smartest things we did was asking for money from someone who did what we did, lived like we lived, had the same stakes in the community we had.

5. If You're Hiring a Leader, Make Them Feel Like One. Once you make a decision to bring someone on board, the next step is to let them do their job. This seems obvious, but I used to have a tough time handing over the reins. However, when we hired someone to run our Ontario expansion, we gave him a bigger office than either George or I had. Might seem like a small thing, but it signalled that this was his territory, his domain, and much was expected of him. As you'll read, that small gesture paid off.

6

WHAT IF I'M WRONG?

On Changing Decisions and Changing Course

"If you never change your mind, why have one?"
—Edward de Bono

If Opportunity Knocks Twice, Let It In

It was 1986, the second time that the world exposition would be held in Canada. The first time was the year of Canada's centennial. Expo '67, in Montreal, is still considered to be the most successful world's fair of the 20th century. Not only was the Expo in Montreal profitable but it also brought an estimated 50 million visitors to the fair grounds—breaking global attendance records—from across the country and around the world. These were the kind of numbers being thrown about by organizers of Expo '86, to be held in Vancouver. How could you not want to be a part of something that big, that important, they asked us. Boston Pizza was one of the first restaurant chains approached because it was a casual dining venue owned by a Canadian company with a particularly high profile in western Canada—just what the organizers wanted. We promised them only one thing: we'd crunch some numbers and look into it.

The stakes were high, but, we'd discover, so was the cost of putting Boston Pizza in the food pavilion. Expo wanted a cool million dollars for three locations: a small takeout place, a medium-sized cafeteria and a full-scale restaurant. To pull that off, we'd have to hire 14 managers and train at least 400 temporary employees. A small army.

George and I had been pondering the idea for almost two years prior. In fact, when it was announced that Vancouver would be the site of Expo '86, we mailed away for the information package about food-service opportunities right away. The pros were obvious. Participating would put Boston Pizza on Vancouver's map, and BC's, not to mention give us exposure to the rest of the world. Participating would also put us in the big leagues with corporate participants like IBM, McDonald's and Coca-Cola.

However, aside from the cost, we were concerned about losing focus. We had just committed to being franchisors, pure and simple. Expo was a marketing tool, and it was temporary. It was an experiment, and we were worried that it could end up being the wrong kind of distraction, the expensive kind, at a very critical time in our growth. After talking about it, meeting about it, writing up countless business plans analyzing it, in the end we decided that we just couldn't afford to drop another million dollars into the venture so soon after borrowing so much to acquire the company. We decided to turn down the opportunity. Besides, we really didn't have the stomach to go back to Bud Grant and Dave Gillespie for yet another million-dollar loan. It was one of those decisions that you make, you feel a little sad about, then you completely let go of. And we knew it was a good decision because it didn't haunt us. But just because you don't regret something doesn't necessarily make it the right decision. It's just perhaps the easiest.

Then Expo organizers came knocking again.

Bill Bennett was premier of the province, and he wanted Expo to be all about BC businesses. Canadian companies were welcome, international ones too, but BC was in a major economic slump, so BC companies were getting the hard sell to participate in this global showcase. The forestry industry was suffering, the Coquihalla Highway construction was ongoing and controversial. It made the Interior, including the Okanagan Valley, more accessible, but environmentalists took issue with its method, its path and its impact on wildlife. Bennett was the target of a lot of loud criticism. He hoped Expo would give the province a morale boost.

After we turned down Expo, we heard rumours that Pizza Hut, an American chain, had approached organizers saying it wanted in. But Bennett was adamant. The whole point of staging Expo in a particular country is to show off that country's wares and boost that country's image. Before entertaining a Pizza Hut offer, Bennett hired Jim Pattison, the billboard billionaire, and Mel Cooper, a radio executive from Newfoundland, to cajole Canadian companies to take part. Mel Cooper was the ultimate salesperson. He burst into our offices one day and just put the gears on us. Boston Pizza was increasingly becoming known as a West Coast success story, he said. Boston Pizza had to make this leap in order for it to grow beyond BC borders, he said. Finally, he said, we sold the kind of food perfectly suited to summertime outdoor eating.

"Think of it," said Mel. "Pizza, beer, soda, sun. You guys gotta do this. You have to find a way."

None of his arguments were new to us. But we kept coming around to the matter of the million-dollar cost.

"I have some flexibility on the matter," said Mel. "Talk to me."

Turns out, deciding to say no put us in a bit of a power position. Over the next hour we negotiated a better deal, one that had Boston Pizza paying the rent from a percentage of our sales, plus we'd get a corporate sponsor title. It didn't budge on the million-dollar fee, but Expo was willing to absorb a little more of the risk. With Expo supporting us so enthusiastically, George felt that we could actually take the plan to a bank and make a strong case to borrow the money. The only thing we needed from our silent partners, Dave and Bud, was for them to back the loan, something they didn't hesitate to do.

We made an appointment at the CIBC, and the four of us slapped on ties.

George had put together yet another attractive financial package that would show the bank how much money we could make in a few months at Expo, and how easy it would be to pay back a million-dollar loan in a few months. By our numbers, and the research sent to us by Expo folks, even if only 15 million visitors came through the grounds, we could easily do $6 million in sales—pretty amazing for a six-month investment.

We were all a little stir-crazy as we waited in the bank lobby for our appointment with the bank manager. During a lull in the conversation, Bud leaned over, snatched the plan from George's hand, scanned the columns and asked about a certain $10,000 fee.

"What's this?"

"That's how much the bank charges for processing the loan," George replied.

"Seriously? And it'll be charging you 8% interest?"

"Yup."

"Would you guys pay *me* that?"

"Uh . . . we'll pay that to whoever lends us the money," said George, glancing over at me.

"Then let's get the hell out of here," Bud said. "Christ, I'll give you guys the goddamn million dollars."

Okay, then. All four of us got up and silently filed past a very confused receptionist and left the CIBC building. To Bud and Dave, that extra million meant they had got in just a little deeper with us. Our partnership was still so new, they weren't sure if they'd made a smart investment with Boston Pizza, however much they might have liked and trusted us. We had yet to prove ourselves. Expo would give them an idea of just what kind of investment they had made.

I was very excited, and I was very nervous.

No Room for Error Means Fewer Errors

Planning Expo was like staging a small, self-contained invasion, with a clear beginning, middle and end. The campaign would begin in January 1986, four months before opening day in May. The Expo closed in October, and we had until December to rip out the facilities and get rid of them. So in a 12-month period we would experience an entire life cycle of a business, without another year to correct any mistakes or make up for the previous year's losses. We'd be in and then out. We'd open a business, then close it. There was no time to tweak the plan. Instead of operating the business on a month-to-month financial cycle, we squeezed it into a weekly financial cycle. Every decision we made at the start of Expo would have to carry us through to the end. The timing was so tight, there was no room for error.

We hired 14 managers and they, in turn, had a week to hire our 400 employees, all culled from Manpower summer applications. We had to buy equipment, ovens and stovetops, but also tables, chairs, forks, knives, napkins and toothpicks. We blew a wad of money on conveyor ovens that could cook an assembly line of pizza rather than one pie at a time. Staff were trained to operate three cafeteria-style locations: a small, a medium and a larger sit-down facility that would show the scope of our menu and abilities. We overcompensated in the personnel department because we were warned to brace ourselves. After all, few had predicted that Expo '67 would be such a smash success. What makes Vancouver any different from Montreal, besides the weather?

Oh right, the weather.

There's a lot to be said about Vancouver, and much of it has to do with weather, which ranges from stunningly beautiful to stunningly bleak, with almost nothing in between.

Opening day, May 2, 1986, it rained. Princess Diana was there with Prince Charles, and then prime minister Brian Mulroney, all huddled under umbrellas, wearing thick winter coats. And it kept on raining the entire first week. And then it rained some more, non-stop, day and night, for two whole months. I kept a little diary that summer, and at the top of every entry was one word: *Rain.* The anticipated massive crowds stayed away in order to stay dry. Every morning I bundled up (it also stayed chilly all spring), grabbed my umbrella and made a tour of the sopping grounds to say hello to our wilted staff. They did their best to keep busy, but it was hard not to catch them standing around bored, shifting their weight from foot to foot, shivering. Manpower didn't send people with a lot of restaurant experience, or much work experience at all, in fact. But even if they didn't shine during the training, we weren't in a position to be picky. We had to make it work with the people we hired. Again, there was no time for second-guessing our early decisions.

When I first took a look at the blueprints of the Expo site, I mentioned to one of the organizers that the sidewalks looked a bit too wide. He assured me that they would be 20, 30 deep in people jammed from side to side. But I couldn't picture it. And now, walking the grounds, the width of the sidewalks made Expo look even more sparsely attended.

By the second week of rain, we had begun to lose money. Keeping the three sites fully staffed was costing more than we were taking in. If the weather kept up, we'd be in trouble.

A month in, we heard other sponsors were starting to aggressively cut back on staff. George and I thought about doing that but decided to hold off for a bit. It had been hard enough to find 400 candidates, then to train them. If we let them go and things turned around, we knew it would become an even bigger disaster. Besides, we had promised the staff jobs all summer and that they'd get paid no matter what. Still, some fled simply from boredom. But of the managers we hired, all but one hung in there.

I tried to hide my concern. During my daily rounds I slapped on a smile and tried to show enthusiasm. Every night, we hovered over a ledger trying to figure out just how much further we could push things before we started to bleed more money. We also used this time to talk to other companies, international ones like IBM and McDonald's, to see how they were handling the sparse crowds and what they were doing to combat the fear. I tried not to think about the million-dollar debt, made worse by the fact that we didn't owe it to a faceless bank but to two guys who believed in us enough to hand us half a business for almost no money of our own down. I'm not a very religious man, but this was around the time both George and I starting praying.

The morning of July 9 I woke up squinting. My eyes hurt. I had fallen asleep with the curtains open, beyond exhausted after another day touring the cold, wet grounds.

This time it was something strange that woke me up. The pain in my eyes was caused by the sunshine flooding my bedroom. I whipped open the sheers, and saw, for the first time in two months, a vivid blue sky. I called George to see if he was seeing the same thing I was.

"It's sunny."

"It is that!"

I bolted down to the Expo grounds.

For the next 56 consecutive days, my daily diary had one word on the top of each page: *Sun.* Vancouver's summer of '86 turned into one of the driest, warmest, sunniest summers on record, and the crowds started to show up. In droves. First, relatively local tourists, in from Seattle and the BC Interior, came to see what Expo was all about. Then folks from around the world who never missed an Expo. Then the crowds of people who came in from Alberta after the Calgary Stampede ended. Then came folks driving all the way from the East Coast of Canada, from Quebec and from Ontario, folks who'd been on the road for days, or weeks, making their last stop the Expo in Vancouver. By September, the final wave consisted of Vancouverites who had been hearing good things about Expo '86 and didn't want to miss out.

We had some mishaps. Once one of the pavilion roofs caved in during the September rains while people were seated in the patio area. No one was hurt, but it was a reminder that the roofs weren't designed to last more than a few months. In the closing weeks, the wear and tear was hard to ignore—including the wear and tear on the staff.

Many of our best employees were students who all went back to school in September. After that, if you could make toast, you had a job at Boston Pizza.

Expo had predicted 15 million people would turn out. But by the end of September, attendance numbers inched closer to 22 million—from 85,000 a day to 350,000. We were serving one person every 20 seconds, including the folks working at BCTV and the sports channel across the way from our 350-seat location. No matter how busy we were, we made sure that those who appeared on TV reporting from the Expo grounds always had a slice of our pizza in their hands. And we were busy. Once we ran out of beer and started selling bottles from the cases we bought for a staff party. On more than one occasion I rolled up my sleeves and became a bartender. Kids who'd never had a job before were getting intensive boot-camp training in restaurant work, from cleaning to making dough to cooking to serving beer. A majority of the temporary managers and sub-managers stayed on with Boston Pizza, some for decades, making the leap from summer employees to long-time staffers. We could barely keep up with the customers streaming in, impatient with the lineups at the other pavilions where staff had been drastically reduced. Money was coming in so fast I hired a full-time counter. A Brinks truck came by every two hours to haul away cash that we stuffed into empty toilet-paper boxes when the cash registers overflowed.

Sales for our three sites topped out at $9 million, 50% more than we originally bargained for. We paid back Bud and Dave with interest and doubled the holiday pay of every employee who stuck with us to the end. The managers who remained for the whole stint received a free Hawaiian vacation.

If You're Going to Fail, Don't Fail Big, Fail Well

The single best decision we made was keeping ourselves fully staffed even when others started to cut costs. We did it because we had commitments and we honoured them. But mostly we decided that if we were going to fail, we'd fail well. Staff, especially trained staff, were a precious commodity. Deciding to cut them loose out of panic and fear would have left us at a serious disadvantage if things turned around. Our thinking was, if attendees were going to choose Boston Pizza over other restaurants, we wanted to make sure they had the entire experience of friendliness and efficiency that came with our great food. Even if they were at some miniature version of our sit-down restaurants, even if they were just enjoying a slice while standing around in the rain, we wanted that experience to be perfect.

After all, wasn't the whole point of Expo to get those attendees into the restaurants *after* Expo? So it was all about service. If we had shaved back staff dramatically and then the rain let up, the crowds would have overwhelmed our remaining pavilions, leaving attendees with a bad taste in their mouths about their Boston Pizza experience. That feeling would carry over to the restaurants. People would associate Boston Pizza with the rushed, harried and inconsistent product they experienced at Expo. And that would affect our company for years to come.

We thought of the million-dollar cost as money we invested to expose the country, and the world, to the Boston Pizza experience, from the venue to the food to the people. It was marketing money; it was the price of doing business in the big leagues. We had to be willing to kiss it goodbye. Making a profit was the hoped-for outcome, but it wasn't a given. The best decision we made was to treat Expo as Boston Pizza's *own* exposition, as our own way of saying, *Here we are, look at us, eat our food, enjoy the atmosphere and keep coming back.* And they did.

In the end, we didn't fail. Quite the opposite. We felt the impact of our successful Expo run almost immediately. We sold a record-breaking 17 franchises the following year. When we signed those cheques to repay Bud and Dave, no one was more surprised at our success than George and me. We had proved things to ourselves that we hadn't even put on the table, including that we could do that kind of volume—some days we took in $250,000, an unthinkable amount of money. We also proved that we could hold our own with the McDonald's of the world.

I remember thinking to myself in Penticton, the year the restaurant did $52,000 in sales, that it'd be great to get to $100,000. Then we surpassed $100,000 in Prince George not long after, and soon we were pulling in $250,000 a year for all three restaurants we had at the time, Prince Rupert included. But to take in $9 million in a few months, in 1-, 5- and 10-dollar bills, well, that's almost indescribable. We had the systems and the recipes and the suppliers and the training. We kept menus simple. We served only beer and wine because we knew it would be mostly families attending the Expo. But I attribute the ability to do that kind of volume to the sheer fact that we got ready, and then we stayed ready.

Also, the excruciating downtime waiting for the rain to end was as beneficial for us as that first dead winter in Penticton; it gave us time to tweak and prepare. We were innovative. We made changes as we went. We did things on the Expo site that we couldn't do in the stores. We started selling pizza slices almost from the get-go when we realized that selling whole or even small pizzas wasn't economical. That meant we had to make really big pizzas in order to be able to cut even wider slices, so we had to change the circumference of our pizza platters. I would never go so far as to say that the rain was a blessing (I had a lot of words for rain that spring of 1986, mostly four-letter ones), but it reinforced my pattern of staying limber during dry periods, of adapting to the circumstances and cutting through fear. In many ways, Expo was my MBA and Boston Pizza's international debut. To say it launched us is an understatement. The timing couldn't have been more perfect. We were ready to set our sights on a bigger market. Much bigger.

Even Small Changes Can Create Big Opportunities

A year before Expo '86, George and I had been invited to an industrial expo in Chiba, Japan. We had never been to Japan, nor anywhere in the Far East, so we were excited. We were feted and chauffeured, and met a lot of great business contacts, some of whom actually came to see what Boston Pizza was all about during our own expo. But Chiba was a business junket, so the organizers packed us onto a charter plane, way in the back near the washrooms. On the way home, the toilets overflowed. We were up to our ankles in pee. It was the worst and longest flight I had ever taken. They eventually moved us to new seats. But it also marked the last time we ever flew coach—a small change that would place someone very important in our path when we made another trip to Asia in January 1987, fresh off the victory of Vancouver's Expo. We had decided to go to Hong Kong to begin making serious inroads into the Asian market.

I had never been to a place like Hong Kong. It was wild, bigger than I could conceive of; a whole new world. Boston Pizza had made a global impression during Expo, and Asia was ripe territory for expansion. I had never seen so many people packed so tightly in such a small geographical area. When we thought of expansion, we were thinking "urban" for the first time. Parking wasn't a consideration, only foot traffic, and no city we visited in Asia was short on that.

Then we went to Taipei, Taiwan, where we found the same incredible density, and where we were whisked around in limos, and taken to great restaurants and nightclubs. American chains were popping up everywhere there. The culture was embracing anything and everything Western. George and I didn't see any reason Boston Pizza couldn't thrive in both Hong Kong and Taiwan. Now we just needed to find the right people to help us break ground.

On the flight back to Vancouver, comfortably seated in

business class, George excused himself to have a cigarette. He was one of those smokers who didn't like sitting in the smoking section. He used to go to the back of the plane and stand in the flight attendant station. While enjoying his cigarette, he watched as an anxious, wiry Chinese man, also seated in business class, burned off energy by pacing up and down the aisles. They struck up a conversation. His name was Clement Ng. George told him we'd been researching the best markets in Asia in which to expand our business. As it turned out, Clement was a Hong Kong investment banker on his way to Vancouver to visit family. He became one of the most valuable contacts we would ever make, all because of a chance encounter on a plane. A few weeks later he came to our headquarters in Richmond, and we went from talking about to actually plotting out our overseas expansion.

Clement met us in Hong Kong a few months later, picking us up at the airport in his Rolls-Royce convertible driven by a chauffeur. That's just how you did business there. Over a seven-year period, Clement was responsible for helping open up China, Hong Kong, Taiwan and Japan to us. He set up meetings with local officials, helped us navigate red tape in order to get Asians to Canada for training and lined up people to staff and run the restaurants on the ground. Doing business in the East is entirely dependent on relationships, on who you know and who, in turn, they know. And everyone seemed to know Clement Ng, including a businessman named Bob Yein, our first franchisee in Asia.

Just Because You're Profitable
Doesn't Mean You're Successful

In those days, to open a franchise from start to finish in Canada took 75 to 90 days if all went well. In Taiwan it took 27 days. There was no workers' compensation board, no insurance concerns. Guys sometimes worked shirtless and barefoot without hard hats, hanging from tippy scaffolding. Even if we wanted to institute safety regulations, there was no way for us to insist on this without embarrassing a supervisor—considered a greater crime than injury on the job. This was a culture where saving face was important. It's still that way. Plus the bureaucracy was beyond Byzantine. Learning new business customs is a never-ending and fascinating process but one that can also be deeply frustrating. We flew back and forth to Asia every four to six weeks, staying for weeks at a time in various countries and cities. We had a bead on everything that was happening in our new territory. Or so we thought.

On Canada Day 1988, we opened our first Boston Pizza in Taipei, a city of more than two million people. From our hotel room at the Grand Hyatt we watched customers line up around the block to eat at the first Canadian-owned restaurant in Taiwan. That morning, getting ready, I caught the Boston Pizza jingle sung in Chinese on the radio! Incredible.

Taipei was unlike the mid-sized Canadian towns that Boston Pizza thrived in. It had a young population working in an aggressive market, who partied until the sun came up, then headed straight to work, where they would shower and change. And they embraced pizza with a kind of enthusiasm matched only by the amount of money they dropped in our restaurant. Almost immediately we made plans to open six more franchises in Taiwan alone, plus one in Japan and one in Hong Kong. By 1992, we had nine stores up and running in Asia. Even Clement Ng, our fixer and go-to guy, became a passionate franchisee.

At first it felt like the right thing to do, to make small changes to better suit this enormous market. Asia was untapped and unknown to us, so we started to listen to our man in China, Bob Yein, who convinced us we had to change some of our key concepts and our menu. We prided ourselves on being open-minded and open to change. We remembered what it was like to be franchisees with a fresh idea that was ignored by headquarters. So we didn't hesitate to follow sound suggestions. We took beer, wine and liquor off the menu, as Boston Pizza was predominately becoming a family restaurant, and booze was too costly to stock and store. We were also told that we shouldn't wrap the face of the store in its iconic bands of red-and-blue neon.

"People will think it's a massage parlour," Bob said.

The store didn't look like a Boston Pizza, and soon the menu didn't resemble it, either. We always offered our standbys—pizza and pasta dishes—but Bob urged us to add Boston Pizza's version of a popular Chinese soup and a Chinese dessert, among other items. We wanted to be successful, and the numbers certainly justified the changes. And we also wanted to be respectful, completely forgetting that Boston Pizza customers were coming for a different experience than they'd get at other Taiwanese restaurants.

Then there was the issue of cleanliness. It's the one thing that'll take down a restaurant faster than poor sales or even a shootout in a bar. If word gets out that your establishment is less than pristine, you're cooked. At least that's the case in Canada and the US. In Taiwan, not so much. So the franchisees had no problem with egg farmers making their deliveries through the front door, or allowing grandma to squat on the kitchen floor to scrub the goo off the eggs with an old rag. Times have changed, but back then, there were no concerns about cross-contamination. If we complained, we'd be told we just didn't "get" how business was done in the East.

But again, we were making money end over end, Japanese yen, new Taiwan dollars, and Hong Kong dollars. And our franchisees had no problem paying the 5% fee. (Unlike franchisees paying 7%, this rate included liquor sales.) To think that we were setting up franchises in cities twice the size of Toronto, cities we had never heard of, in a formerly closed country, was incredible.

Then in 1989 came Tiananmen Square, the deadly months-long uprising in Beijing that saw students rallying for greater economic freedom. The media were concentrated in Beijing, but what outsiders didn't know was that these protests were all over Asia; I saw versions in Hong Kong, Shanghai, and Taiwan, not just Tiananmen Square. Everywhere we went, crowds were calling for more liberalization and greater reform. And the army was close by. It was a tense time to be a Westerner there. You got mixed reactions from Asians about growing a Western business in China, depending on what side of the political or philosophical divide they fell on. Walls were crumbling in some places as fast as they were being built up in others. It was often hard to know which way the tide was turning. Sometimes, flying into Taiwan, we'd be told to shut the blinds. The Taipei airport shared space with the local air force, and the government didn't want spies taking pictures from above.

I had come to know and love Taiwan. In fact, I believe there is no more entrepreneurial a people on the planet than the Chinese, a result perhaps of strict Communism, which forces people to find ingenious ways to make a little more money, and starve a little less. I've seen farmers with 500-square-foot plots grow enough to feed their family for a year and sell some food on the side for a tidy profit. You have to remember, this is a civilization that's tens of thousands of years old. George and I would take whole afternoons off to wander the Chiang Kai-shek Memorial in Taipei. We were told there were so many artifacts stored in the museum's warehouse that it could rotate its exhibit every week for 10 years and you wouldn't see the same thing. Here we were, two small-town boys from Canada, looking at thousands and thousands of years of Chinese history. Boston Pizza and other Western businesses were a teeny, tiny, infinitesimal part of this ever-changing world. We never failed to be moved or astonished by that. You could hardly keep up with its evolution. One day I'd be standing on a balcony of a hotel in Shanghai, admiring the water buffalo grazing on the shores along the Bund. A few years later, same hotel, same balcony, but the water buffalo were replaced by rows and rows of high-rises, a new one opening every day. Instead of paying my waiter in the local currency, I'd be handing him my American Express card. Asia moves that fast.

Being Available Isn't the Same as Being Committed

So Boston Pizza should have been an unmitigated success in Asia. The continent was ripe for westernization, the people were enterprising, the market getting stronger and stronger. But by 1994, six years after the first Boston Pizza opened its doors to great fanfare, we closed the last of nine restaurants and went home. What happened? We were making wads of money, and we proved that there was a terrific appetite for pizza and pasta in the East. And there was an incredible labour pool available to staff the restaurants. But we weren't focused. While building up in Asia, we were also opening several stores in Ontario—in Windsor, Newmarket and Brampton. We weren't capitalized enough in either place to ensure solid on-the-ground support. We had spread ourselves too thin and didn't have the support systems in place to manage the massive, rapid growth. We had no offices in Asia and none in Ontario. We flew in and out, over and over, thinking we could hire talented people to handle the local issues, while we managed the bigger picture from Vancouver. We'd never been more wrong with any single decision we'd made up until that point. We clearly didn't have a handle on the Asian expansion. When we finally discovered that Bob hadn't secured long-term leases, which began doubling and tripling in cost as they came up for renewal, we knew it was time to fold the restaurants and regroup.

At the same time, our expansion into Ontario was flailing. As a franchisor, we began to realize that we had to lead, not follow. But in order to lead, we had to physically be there. We made that mistake in Asia, and we were starting to feel the effects of long-distance management in Ontario too. In fact, one of our franchisees, carefully selected because of his experience as a vice-president of a big corporation, had a massive meltdown on opening day. He called me in a panic—not from the restaurant but from the basement of his house, where he had fled to.

"Jim, I can't do this. I can't handle it. It's too busy," he said. Instead of tackling the crowds and managing the flow, he got into his car and drove home. "I'm not cut out for this work, man."

I urged him to get back in his car and go show some backbone on the floor. It was not a time to panic and run. Problem was, I was in Vancouver. But his mind was shut to advice, and he became entrenched, unable to budge from his house. There was nothing I could do to help him. I called the restaurant and tried to coach and consult from thousands of kilometres away, but it was madness to do business like that.

Being thousands of kilometres away also meant we didn't have a clue what was really going on in the rest of our Ontario stores. Another franchisee had installed a giant smoker in his kitchen, without clearing it with us or the insurance company. Another put hot dogs for kids on the menu, with no consistent controls over who supplied the meat.

Then came the dreaded GST, a new tax that would affect restaurants, among many things. On top of the usual 10% to 15% tip, diners were also being asked to pay the new 7% tax, making eating out a bigger luxury than it had ever been before. Then, of course, there was a PST in Ontario, which added another 8%. So we were basically asking diners to add about 30% to every bill. It proved to be a very tough adjustment. We weren't the only restaurant to take a hit over this. Business was down across the board.

In 1992, we did the only thing we could do at the time: we closed shop as soon as possible. When the leases and the franchise agreements came up, we didn't renew them. Again, we came to the tough and radical decision to pull out of Ontario. It had been an expensive mistake. One of our franchisees had borrowed almost half a million dollars from the bank to open a Boston Pizza. I flew to Toronto for a meeting with the bank to show him support, and I'll never forget the bank manager's sneering tone.

"Look," he said, "you have a nice little western business. Why don't you just go back to BC and keep it that way?"

I felt like I was being run out of town on a rail. I was 47. For the first time in my life I contemplated retirement. Instead, I took a long vacation to Hawaii, something I hadn't done in years. I didn't plan to do much but golf and tan, but instead I found myself pacing a lot and talking to George on the phone. If I had any serious thoughts of retiring early, they were erased after spending the afternoon on the golf course with a bunch of retirees, who complained non-stop about their pensions. I didn't want that to be me. My eight-week vacation lasted one week. Soon I was back on a plane to Vancouver to reassess and regroup—but not before taking the time to assess the expanding and contracting nature of our company.

Was it the wrong decision to expand into Ontario and Asia? No. But it was the wrong decision to expand in both directions at the same time. It was also wrong not to set up an office in each location first and hire staff to support overseas local franchisees. We thought that flying in and out of town was sufficient supervision. We thought we had good local managers on the ground. In other words, we thought we could get away with doing it the cheap way. But by managing from afar we came to compromise our brand at every turn, from nixing neon in Beijing to serving hot dogs in Ontario. By not being on the ground to catch these inconsistencies, we let our brand get trampled by managers who didn't have Boston Pizza's interests in mind, only their own. In many ways, you can't blame them. I'm not excusing managers who bilked us or took advantage of us. But many of our Asian franchisees felt those restaurants were *their* restaurants, not ours. It was *theirs* to do with as they pleased because the bigger entity, the head office, was in faraway Canada. So we might as well have not existed at all.

We had also made the grievous decision of changing our concept to suit the location, rather than finding the right location to suit our concept. We didn't listen to our gut when people told us to get rid of our neon. We shouldn't have tampered with the menu. We should have trusted that the local tastes would embrace us if we stayed true to our winning formulas and recipes. But the biggest mistake we made was not overseeing Bob Yein more closely. We soon discovered he was franchising a number of our competitors, and using profits from Boston Pizza to operate a chain of nightclubs.

Bob wasn't doing anything illegal, but he was acting in his own best interests at every turn, and not in Boston Pizza's. He had no loyalty to us because we weren't there supporting him and steering him. He didn't owe us any allegiance.

You might be asking if it would have been easier to just remove Bob Yein, leave the restaurants up and running, and set up a local office to support them (better late than never), rather than close down. However, the leases weren't in our name. They were in Bob Yein's. This was deliberate: we didn't want to guarantee the lease. But that meant we didn't have any control over the length of those leases, and we couldn't negotiate for better rates. And the prices went up. When the leases expired, the lease holders charged prices only banks could afford. We closed down our locations, profitability be damned.

If the Wheel Works, Why Reinvent It?
The Ontario and Asia expansion, and all the initial missteps that followed, changed the way we decide on fran-

chisees. Money is key, obviously. You have to be financially capable of taking on the risk. Back in the 1980s, the initial franchise fee was about $15,000—and you needed another $500,000 or so to build and open a restaurant. Today's one-time franchise fee is about $60,000—but it costs more than a million to open the restaurant. Our yearly percentage hasn't changed: it's 7% of sales (excluding alcohol). In exchange we provide eight weeks of restaurant and marketing training, which includes leadership seminars for the senior management running the kitchen and the floor. We also provide in-house support for the restaurant during the first month of operation as the franchise finds its legs and relaxes into its role. There are cost advantages as well.

Head office negotiates on behalf of a national, and sometimes international, company for certain products, whether it's sauce, flour or soft drinks, so supply costs are lower. An independent restaurant would pay considerably more for those items because they're one-off purchases. We buy in huge volumes and can get huge discounts. Also, formulas and recipes have been thoroughly tested to see what works and what doesn't. Everything is fine-tuned to perfection. Every franchise has something to teach the others. That collective wisdom takes the mystery out of a business plan, which gives a franchisee a lot of confidence out of the gate.

As a franchise group, it's also cheaper to advertise. We do something called cooperative advertising. Every franchise pays a small portion of a national or international ad campaign. It's cheaper than running ads for individual franchises, plus it reinforces the idea that we are a big, international company, with a consistent, singular, quality brand.

Boston Pizza boasts some of the lowest food costs in the industry, about 25%; other chains hover in the 30% range. Why? Pasta and pizza are mostly just flour. And we buy in bulk for all of our supplies, from tomatoes to toilet paper to toothpicks. And because our food preparation process isn't complicated—no intricate recipes—we don't need to employ highly trained chefs. We just need skilled people who can be consistent, dedicated and thorough. That keeps labour costs down as well, which is why a Boston Pizza can make a go of it in small towns and the suburbs.

It's nice to run a successful independent restaurant, but the failure rate for one-offs is high. The fact is, people—especially in non-urban areas—are less likely to spend money at a restaurant they're unfamiliar with. Franchise-owned restaurants are consistent: you know what to expect, and you'll likely get a good deal for your dollar.

We've come a long way from Greek statues and a handful of scribbled recipes. Boston Pizza is a brand, and we don't mess with that anymore. Once we figured out what we were, what we offered and what people had come to expect from their experience with the restaurant, we institutionalized it. The early expansion into Asia and Ontario taught us that the more we tampered with the brand, the more trouble we got into. Today, we know we have a tested model, one that's been successful in other markets, and prospective franchisees come in knowing they can make it fly in theirs.

Hire for Fit

Not every great restaurateur can be great at running a franchise. Credentials are important, and we give preference to franchisees with at least five years of casual dining experience. (Their silent partners may be lawyers or accountants or whatever.) But I just know in my gut if someone is a people person or a business person, two very different animals. And because I go into the office every day, I've absorbed Boston Pizza's culture into my DNA. I know who'll blend in and who might become an irritant. But I learned this the hard way.

We sold a franchise to a successful BC businessman and his wife. They had the money and experience in running a franchise after operating a local gas station for several years. Now they wanted to get into the restaurant business. They passed the financial scrutiny, and although I did have some concerns about the husband's shyness, his wife sparkled, and I hoped her outgoing personality would counterbalance his introverted one. I was wrong.

After a great start, their sales stagnated, then plummeted. Then we began to receive complaints. One was from a group of parents travelling on a bus through town with their kids' soccer team. When they pulled in for supper at the Boston Pizza, the franchisee made them eat in shifts—kids first, then the parents. The husband's reasoning? He didn't want to move the tables. He wanted to keep the layout of the restaurant intact and serve in shifts. That, to us, was unacceptable service, and an indication that there was something fundamentally wrong with the store's culture.

Accommodating a customer's needs is at the heart of what any good restaurant does; the best ones anticipate them. That's what we've always strived for.

I got on a plane to see what was up with that store.

Pulling in, I thought the place was spotless, the exterior polished to perfection, not a weed poking through the concrete of the parking lot. This franchisee would likely have won every award for cleanliness, from the foyer to the deep-freeze. That's a good thing. We love cleanliness. But this veered into the antiseptic and unwelcoming, the way some homes leave you feeling like you can't touch anything. Like no one lives there.

The atmosphere inside was dead. The franchisee was so focused on running a clean, tight ship, he forgot that actual people were involved in the operation. Ultimately, I discovered, this guy was people-adverse, a deadly quality to possess if you work in a restaurant. He spent most of this time holed up in his office, looking over ledgers, and no time on the floor meeting and greeting guests or interacting with staff. I had a feeling that if we didn't do something soon, we'd have to shutter the restaurant.

Those are tricky situations. It's hard to change a person's fundamental nature. If you're not a people person, you're just not. So we took a radical approach and found a partner for them who had all the gregarious qualities the husband lacked. We urged the franchisee to sell the new partner half the business and let him try to turn things around. The situation was dire enough that the couple was willing to try anything. Within no time, the place was packed and humming again, and it soon became clear that the original franchisees were not built for the restaurant business. They were soon bought out. That franchise is now one of the biggest earners in the Boston Pizza family.

Our initial, ill-fated expansion into Asia and Ontario taught us to spend the money and go in ahead of time, well ahead of opening even one franchise. Get to know the country, the county, the city, the town and the neighbourhood. Identify its rhythms, its industries, its eating patterns, its experts, its competition and its traffic schedules. Think about sourcing supplies locally; in Asia, we can do that better today than back in the 1980s. Back then in China, we couldn't find the flour we needed to make the pasta and pizza dough, never mind the tomato sauce and special toppings. We had to ship it all there, which was incredibly costly. Today, there are more options. When it comes to flour and tomatoes, we could also go the route of Starbucks, which has begun to grow its own coffee beans in China, rather than pay to ship them over.

To Know a Place Is to Know Its Traffic

When we decided to re-enter Ontario, we treated the province like a foreign country about which we had a lot to learn. I had to think like an Ontarian. I went back to my police training, back to the principles in which I was trained. Want to crack open a case? Immerse yourself in the details of the case. Want to find a suspect? Put yourself in a suspect's shoes—a lesson I put to use one night during a foot chase. It was winter in Prince George; colder than the north side of a polar bear's ass. My partner and I split up to cover more ground. I must have sprinted a half a mile after that suspect. I thought I had him cornered at the end of a long, dark alley, but it was as if he'd just disappeared into thin air. I was a non-smoker and only in my early 20s, but the cold air and chase had me doubled over with my hands on my knees, gasping. Then it dawned on me that if I was choking after that sprint, the suspect must be too. I held my breath until all was perfectly still and silent. I waited a beat . . . and sure enough, I could hear the suspect panting on the other side of the fence, just inches away. I reached over and easily grabbed him by the scruff of the neck.

The rhythm of living in Ontario is a little different from that of living in BC. The first clue came on a Saturday morning, as I woke up in my hotel room in downtown Toronto. I was in for work, but there was a weekend Blue Jays game that I wanted to see. I called around for some tickets, which, I discovered, were slightly easier to find than someone to go with me to the game. There wasn't a soul in town. Everyone I knew was at a place called Muskoka, which I hadn't heard of before. In the Okanagan, we upped the staff on the weekends because the Okanagan was the weekend destination—it was the Muskoka of BC. This knowledge about Ontario would now inform when we set up meetings and booked conferences, and certainly where we could set up franchises. Weekends at Boston Pizza are all about the patio, so no use putting franchises in places we knew would be vacant for those prime summer months.

Also, Ontarians have two things that didn't exist in BC at

the time, and still don't to the same degree: shift work and rush hour, especially in the Golden Horseshoe. Meals are planned around shift changes and traffic. If you worked the seven-to-three shift at the Ford plant in Oakville, by the time you picked up your kids from school or daycare, got home and took a shower, you were hungry. You wanted dinner. And it was only five o'clock in the afternoon. So, people in Ontario generally eat earlier because their days start much earlier. This changed the way we staffed our Ontario restaurants, which often got slammed at 6 p.m., a full two hours earlier than the busiest seating in BC.

Here's something else to gnaw on: there were more Italians in Ontario than in BC, so you'd think launching a pizza franchise would be a no-brainer. But I didn't know until much later that most Italians prefer tomato sauce to meat sauce. And if they do eat meat sauce, they call it "bolognese," a term we didn't use at Boston Pizza.

In BC we used deck ovens, with multiple baking chambers, because customers tended to trickle into the dining room, and you can get away with cooking pizzas one at a time. In Ontario, people arrived in clusters, slamming the dining room in shifts, so we began to install conveyor ovens instead.

The early 1990s aren't so long ago, but even then, most of the companies in Canada were either western- or eastern-based. There were no Boston Pizzas in Ontario, just as in BC there were no Swiss Chalets or East Side Mario's. Earls and White Spot were as popular in Vancouver as Kelsey's was in Toronto. Only The Keg was making a real go of it in both BC and Ontario, though it occupied a niche part of the market called "luxury casual." It was as though an invisible boundary cut Canada in half, with very little franchise traffic flowing in the east-west direction. There were no national chains in what's known as the mid-scale segment. (The other two segments are quick serve, where you'll find the McDonald's and KFCs, and fine dining, which are usually local.) Even Starbucks was years away from opening in the east. I remember my first time ordering a coffee at a Tim Hortons in Oakville. My companion ordered a "double double." I take my coffee black but said, "Me too," thinking "double" had something to do with doubling up the cardboard lining for a hot cup. One milky, sugary sip later I was spitting out my coffee into the shrubs. Being from the west, I wasn't familiar with Tim's restaurant lingo any more than my companion had heard of White Spot's Triple "O" sauce, or a Starbucks grande skinny latte.

Fail Once, Fear Less

Rick Arndt, a franchisee and Edmonton architect we hired to redesign the restaurant, joined me on several reconnaissance trips through Ontario. He was five foot four to my six foot four. We were quite the pair. We didn't have a clear plan of action. We flew into Toronto and rented a car. We asked around for suggestions for places to eat, or we'd just happen upon a place, taking note of what made us stop. Was it because it was in a convenient location? Did we like the look of the building? Did it seem friendly, clean and approachable? Was the parking convenient? What about the colours? The neon? The sign? Was it warm or forbidding? It wasn't even really about the food, as that was something we were less concerned about tweaking at Boston Pizza. There had been some rumblings among our franchisees to lose the word "pizza" and just call the restaurant "Boston's," but we held tight to the idea that pizza was the mainstay around which the rest of the menu revolved. What I always liked about the idea of pizza is its experience—that a bunch of people, family or friends, gather around a table sharing a dish that they all put thought into. It sets the tone of the evening, regardless of whether you even actually order pizza.

What were we looking for on those reconnaissance trips? Just a sense of what worked for restaurants in the east. We drove from northern Ontario to Windsor in the south to find it. We broke our trips up, doing a week in Toronto, eating at some restaurants, scoping out the exteriors of others. Then we'd fly home. A couple weeks later, we'd go to Ottawa and drive to Montreal, a city that loves to eat out. I'd note a particular shade of yellow at a popular Italian restaurant in Toronto. We'd pass a suburban steakhouse like Outback and notice how its neon made it look a little dated. All the while, Rick made sketches.

It became pretty clear it wouldn't be good enough to fly in and out of Ontario. One of us had to actually move there. Rick and I were both dyed-in-the-wool western Canadian boys. We had deep roots in the Prairies and the Rockies, and no real affinity for flat Ontario, let alone Toronto's centre-of-the-universe attitude. (I'd discover that this was more reputation than reality.) But we knew it wasn't enough to assume that just because something worked in one part of the country it naturally would thrive in another.

At the time, I was ending a brief second marriage to a woman named Bronwyn Tolley, so a move to Ontario was, after some consideration, welcome. I hoped a relocation could get me focused on something other than my home life. I tip my hat to George and his wife, Sylvia, whose marriage has weathered the growth of the company, and survived the travel, the long hours and the constant distractions.

Turned out the move was a blessing. It was in Ontario that I finally got to know a woman named Sandi Beauchamp. We had met briefly at the Atlanta Olympics, when we exchanged business cards on a junket. I was immediately impressed with her, plus she had a business background that also involved travel, long hours and constant distraction. She gets me, and she understands my industry. Life with me is not always easy, but in Sandi I have found a true partner.

Once Rick and I nailed a new look for Boston Pizza, he flew back to his offices in Edmonton and began drawing up options and sketching out floor plans. The next step was to find someone to run operations in Ontario. I didn't quite know how to describe the job, as we'd never had this sort of office set-up before, but it would be local management that would be self-contained, handling everything in Ontario and eventually Atlantic Canada that BC handled out west.

Be Cautious but Not Too Cautious

Through an expensive headhunter, whose offices looked like a turn-of-the-19th-century bordello, we found the perfect candidate in Mark Pacinda. The hiring process can take weeks, even months. But I met Mark on a Thursday, George flew out to meet him the following Tuesday, and we hired him the next day. By then, George and I had honed our selection process down to an art. We just knew in our gut that Mark was the right guy for the job. And we were right. He's been with us ever since.

After a handshake at the velvet-lined headhunter's office, we began taking regular meetings in my new office, a small tippy table at a Starbucks in Oakville, near the home Sandi and I now shared. Mark had seen Boston Pizza restaurants on trips out west, but he knew little about our company and its history. I brought him up to speed and tried to describe what exactly he'd be establishing in Ontario. He wouldn't be running the restaurants, I explained; he'd be supporting them. He'd be looking for the right franchisees, helping with local marketing and scoping out real estate. The head office would still be in Richmond, BC. It would still do the buying and ordering. It would still make all the big decisions affecting each franchise. But the Ontario office would handle Ontario concerns.

"I'm not quite sure what the office will be called, but you'd run it," I said.

"Sounds like you want to set up a BMU in Ontario," he said.

"What's a BMU?" These were times when my lack of

MBA, let alone university education, was apparent. I had no idea what he was talking about.

"Business management unit. A local head office that's charged with locally growing, promoting and supporting the franchises in the region."

"Yeah. That's what I want. Exactly that."

I laugh when I think about it today. That's me in a nutshell: all instinct. I knew what I wanted, and what the company needed, before I even knew there was a name for it. (We now have three regional offices, or BMUs: one in Richmond, BC, one in Mississauga, Ontario, and one in Laval, Quebec.)

Mark had recently moved to Canada from Sydney, Australia, where he'd helmed the Kentucky Fried Chicken franchises. He'd also been president of Arby's Canada. Both were multi-billion-dollar global corporations I admired, with thousands of existing stores. Boston Pizza, meanwhile, had nothing set up in Ontario, no franchises there, no offices other than my regular table at Starbucks, and a shoddy track record from the last time it was in the province. When Mark told a friend of his that he'd taken a job with a restaurant company that had no restaurants in the area he was in charge of, his friend replied, "Basically, you have an imaginary job."

But Mark wanted to be part of something truly entrepreneurial, a real start-up, because that's the only way to describe what we were doing. Boston Pizza might have been a very successful western enterprise, but in Ontario we were just breaking ground and starting from scratch.

We went back there with the attitude that we weren't afraid to fail. What was there to be afraid of? We had failed once before and we survived. If it all went to pot, we'd survive again. We weren't cocky, but we were also not overly cautious.

While Ontario head offices were being built in Mississauga, we hit the ground running, starting with advertising in franchising magazines and setting up booths at trade shows where potential franchisees came to find new opportunities. A franchisee is a certain kind of entrepreneur: rather than coming up with an original idea—which is always hit or miss—he or she knows how to spot a good thing and wants to ride the wave. The rule of thumb is, you have to meet 10 franchisees or franchising groups in order to close one deal, so we met a lot of people, many of whom were skeptical about Boston Pizza making another go of it in Ontario. No franchise restaurant had ever done that: closed up shop, only to reopen just a few years later. But this time, we explained, we were not only going to do things differently, we were also going to look completely different.

A few months after hiring Mark, I set him up in our new offices. I made sure my office was the smallest in the suite, Mark's the biggest. I wanted Mark to feel that he ruled that roost. This was his place, Ontario his domain, his part of the empire to grow. Then we called a general meeting in Edmonton at Rick Arndt's architectural firm.

By then, Rick and I had come up with a dozen concept drawings of what the new Boston Pizza was going to look like, and we pinned them to the walls of a big conference room. We were strategic. We had already decided which one *we* liked the best, so we lined up the pictures, promenading the staff past all the other okay potentials, saving the drawing we loved the most for last. Everyone loved our choice. It had a creamy yellow facade, with a red-capped rooftop circled in red lights. It had wide rectangular windows and a warmly lit interior. It looked both upscale and inviting. We dumped the dull brick exteriors and any remnants of Greek kitsch or faux ethnic tablecloths and curtains. The new interiors would be painted a deep red, and have plush booths and low-hanging light fixtures. We wanted it to look like the most inviting room of your home, a combination kitchen and family room. The only thing we'd preserve was the iconic blue and red "BP" logo, which hung like a clock in the tower above the front doors. Everyone was dazzled. It was like a rebirth.

George has this saying, "A successful restaurant company starts with a successful restaurant." A lot was riding on Nepean. It would set the tone and tempo for our Ontario expansion and points east. We opened on September 22, 1998. It was a smaller unit, about 5,000 square feet—1,000 square feet smaller than our average store out west. So we were hoping for $40,000 in sales the first week. We would have been happy with that. It was the average, and we might have settled for a little less, since it was a smaller venue.

The first week of sales was $60,000. That's when we knew. We were back.

After the success of Nepean, we built a Boston Pizza in Oakville that would act as our corporate store where we trained people and tested new products and recipes. George and I also had to alter our communication strategy, which previously had consisted, for the most part, of just having lunch together every day. I knew what he was going to order before he even sat down. Now we were living in different provinces and different time zones, so we had to schedule conversations, and we had to fly in to meet face to face on a regular basis. We let that lapse a few times, to our detriment. Ours is a partnership that doesn't work if we're not booking face time. I love technology, and we both embrace every new software and gadget that enhances communication, but nothing beats sitting down over a coffee and hashing things out in person. And we've committed to that. After all, leaving notes was the death knell of my partnership with Don Spence.

Eighteen months into our Ontario expansion, we knew we were getting a good foothold. We developed a new strategy we called an "area development model" whereby rights were sold to franchisee groups that already owned clusters of Boston Pizzas in other provinces. They have the financial ability and the expertise to develop a whole territory at once, in this case Ontario. That's how we went from zero stores in 1998 to 109 just 14 years later. For a long time, Alberta was home to the most Boston Pizza franchises. In 2009, that number tipped to Ontario. I often think of that bank manager who in told me to leave Ontario and not bother coming back. Keep your West Coast business on the west coast, and let Ontario grow its own franchises, he said. I don't like "I told you so." I don't like to dwell on that kind of sentiment, but I've got to tell you, it feels damn good to have proved him wrong.

But really, it's about the customer's profile. In the suburbs, we build with kids and families in mind. Wider aisles can accommodate strollers, and each is stocked with colouring books and high chairs. In our few urban locations, we build for the bar experience. We want it to be a place where 20-somethings can hang out and have a beer. But hopefully those very same urban customers will stay with us once they head to the suburbs in a few years and start having kids.

We've done well in the suburbs, building on almost every lot where you can find big box stores and giant AMC theatres. That expansion in the early 2000s was aggressive and well timed. But I'm excited about getting more Boston Pizzas into urban locations like downtown Toronto. It takes a little more time to find the right real estate. Parking is always an issue; there's never enough. But foot traffic and accessible public transportation make up for it in a big way. In June 2011, we opened our first downtown Toronto location in the CBC building, 10 floors below where *Dragons' Den* is shot. It feels like we've come full circle. This Boston Pizza is an entirely different-looking franchise; it's modern with a glass, leather and wood interior. But it's still a place where you can grab a beer with friends and catch the game.

You Can Change an Experience
without Changing the Brand

Next territory on our agenda was Quebec. It's like a country within a country, with its own culture that extends beyond language. Because we were sensitive to these differences, it took us a while to find our first location. In fact, we had a marketing specialist and senior managers established in Quebec long before we had the first franchise up and running. When I say "established," I mean these guys were working and living in Quebec. We learned from our China mistake, and we treated Quebec like it was a unique country, and we were right to do that. Plus we had enough humility to know that we knew very little about doing business in that province. Our on-the-ground team was on an extended reconnaissance mission, digging, researching, driving around, eating in competing restaurants near and far from our desired location. They were charged with finding out exactly what it took to be a restaurateur in a province that loves its cuisine. One of my closest friends from my police days was Hector Chamberlain. We stayed in touch, and I remembered a bit of advice he gave me when I told him Boston Pizza was thinking of expanding into Quebec.

"Keep it a Boston Pizza, but make it 'French,' Jim. The whole experience."

What he meant was hire locally, answer the phone in French and translate the entire menu. Quebeckers like a longer lunch and tend to order full bottles of wine at noon (bless them), so we changed the menu accordingly. They also eat soup and salad separately. Plus we added poutine and *tarte au sucre* to the menu, while maintaining the core items—pizza and pasta—that define Boston Pizza. Something else unique to our Quebec franchises is singing. Every morning, the staff sing a morale-boosting song that changes week to week. Even customers get in on the tradition. It's unique to those stores, and it's one of my favourite things about them. We didn't bring that tradition to Boston Pizza, but it's a tradition that sprouted organically in our Quebec stores and we encourage it.

I attribute the rapid growth and success not only to Mark Pacinda and our talented franchisees but also to the decision we made for me to move to Ontario and be on the ground. It was a move I was to repeat again in 2001, this time to Dallas, when it came time for us to penetrate one of the most difficult markets on the planet, the US. It's the big "of course," isn't it? Expanding into the States is considered by many entrepreneurs to be the logical next step. And here's the reasoning, which I've heard so often on *Dragons' Den: I've got a great product. It's doing well in Canada, but what will really put me over is getting a foothold in the States. I'm here for money to enter the US market. So I can sell a lot more of what I've got. I mean, how different can the markets be? Don't you just make the decision to expand to the States and then do it?* They think their only problem is lack of customers, and the only solution is finding them in the US.

I'll admit that was me before I actually made a go of it, before I hit the kind of roadblocks I had never seen before. Like those entrepreneurs who thought the US market was

an "of course," I'd seen other successful franchises strad-
dling the border and I'd think, why can't we find the same
success in the States that we enjoy in Canada? How different are we, really? How hard can it be?

Harder than I ever imagined.

Checklist for Decisions about Growth and Expansion

Twice Boston Pizza found itself in big trouble: at the end of our first winter in Penticton and in those early months during Expo '86. In both of those instances, we didn't overreact, we didn't panic. We buckled down and waited out the weather. So it's easy to look back on triumph and say that going to Expo was the right decision. Maybe so. But it wasn't the best decision we made. The best decision we made was not cutting back on staff when we could have, when the numbers screamed that we, in fact, should have. When we decided to push it well past the date other venues began to cut staff to save money, we unknowingly gave ourselves an edge. Then it was luck that brought out the sun, and the wisdom of that decision became apparent. And I've since come to realize invaluable lessons from our big upheavals, lessons that continue to guide me:

1. Never Mess with the Brand. We compromised our vision in Asia and in Ontario, and could have lost control of the business. That's how it happens. I remember talking to the president of Wardair, the now defunct airline. We were at some ceremony or other, and he turned to me and said, "Jim, I think I've lost control of my company." He used to know the name of all the crews, down to the last flight attendant. But his company grew fast, too fast, and it entered the commercial market, which he was unfamiliar with. Wardair was about charters, and he said he should have grown more in that market before branching out into the commercial space, where competition is fierce and the market unpredictable.

I think this also applies to me. I'm a brand—in many respects, we all are. To make a leap and overcome my fear of being on TV, I told myself that I just had to be myself. That was my only job. I had to trust that the producers wanted me, my brand, and not some other version of me. And I have to remind myself of that all the time, whenever I'm tempted to be any different from what I am. That takes away the fear. After all, I can only be me. That has to be enough.

2. Retreat Is Not Defeat. Whether it's expanding too slowly, too quickly, way ahead of your time or a little too late, there are a million reasons why something doesn't work in a new territory. Once we figured out why we were in trouble in Asia and Ontario, the only smart decision was to shut down, get out and regroup. In situations like that, decisions are best made with a clean start in mind, not a fix. The entire entry into the market was flawed. It required a new plan. We never doubted that those two territories (Ontario and Asia) would be in our crosshairs again; it was just a matter of when.

3. Reactions Aren't Decisions. That's an important distinction. Reactions are usually actions taken in haste and made with fear. A decision is a plan—without the action. Ideally, there is a small space between a decision and the action that follows, which will allow for tweaking. You can't often take that time as a police officer, but you sure as hell better as a leader.

192

4. Only Listen to Someone Who's Been There. Consultants are a dime a dozen. If you want to know how to make it in your industry, look to the people who are doing it. Ask *them* questions and follow *their* advice. Look into mentorship programs. Join clubs where you'll meet people in your industry. If you're not a joiner or a people person, rethink being an entrepreneur. So much of your success will depend on building relationships, often within your own community.

5. Plants Can't Take Root in Two Places. Making the decision to expand is one of the most crucial aspects of a business. Building in Asia and Ontario wasn't the problem; building both at the same time was. Keep growth small at first. Expand near, then far. Not a lot of companies can conquer far-flung territories at the same time. It's like waging a battle on several fronts. It's doable, but it's complicated, and you leave your company extremely vulnerable. I like focus. And I like organic growth, which starts from the epicentre of the operation and moves out in consecutive waves. That's what I love about Frogbox, a franchise that rents big, stackable, reusable moving boxes that are picked up from and then delivered to homes. Its growth started in the west, is inching east, and will grow south to the states nearest to the Canadian border.

In Boston Pizza's case, after pulling out of Asia and Ontario, we grew steadier from BC to the Prairie provinces, re-entering Ontario, then spreading east from Quebec to Newfoundland. That's how we've become the only

Canadian restaurant chain in our category that's in all of the provinces and two of the three territories. Even The Keg can't boast that. Tim Hortons doesn't count—it falls in the fast food category, not casual dining.

From there we spring-boarded into the US, and our growth will head along north-south parameters before we even consider heading to Asia again. It's a road map that's really working this time. But I can sum up our strategy in three short sentences: Keep it simple. Grow it slowly. Start near, then go far.

7

HOW DO YOU KNOW YOU'RE READY TO GROW?

Making Decisions in Uncertain Times

"Never be afraid to try something new. Remember, amateurs built the ark; professionals built the Titanic.*"*
—Unknown

Every Lion Begins as a Cub

It was the mid-1990s, and I was golfing in Palm Springs with a guy named Rob Fix. He was trying to sell me a membership at his club. He had a lot of charisma, and he was doing a pretty good job. I have a knack for spotting a good salesperson, so I turned the tables and began interviewing *him*.

"Ever thought of selling something other than golf memberships?"

"Like what?"

"Restaurant franchises."

Soon after, I signed him on. We opened a small satellite office in Palm Springs. If people inquired about opening a franchise in the US, we sent them Fix's way. He would do the preliminary work, which involved mostly just figuring out if prospective franchisees could get properly financed. Back then, money was easier to come by than it is now, that's for sure.

In 1998, we opened our first American franchise in Tempe, Arizona. It wasn't a hard sell. A franchisee in Calgary who spent winters in Tempe thought it was a ripe market, and he was right. But he didn't open a Boston Pizza. He opened a Boston's The Gourmet Pizza, our name in the US. Turned out "Boston Pizza" was being used by a few companies in a few states. You'd think it would be a disaster to have to register a new name for a popular restaurant established in another country. But it wasn't. No matter what our restaurants were called, we were still completely new to Americans. We were still starting from scratch. And I mean from scratch: we were starting from the very beginning, as we had in the Penticton days, putting aside all of our experience since then.

After we trademarked the name Boston's The Gourmet Pizza, Boston Chicken—which became Boston Market— came after us right away. For years, we'd been successful at keeping it out of Canada, so naturally when we announced plans to expand into the US, the restaurant, now owned by McDonald's, sued us. In response, we did what you're expected to do in the States: we sued back. At one point, even our lawyers asked us if we really wanted to push the issue. They suggested we back down and maybe drop "Boston" from our name. But the discussion was a non-starter. We weren't going to give up on "Boston," and we weren't going to back down. The other restaurant quickly got the message that this was a fight we weren't walking away from. It took a couple of years but, eventually, we came to terms over territory and name use. This was an eye-opener, and it served as our "Welcome to America."

We were still rapidly growing the Ontario market, so I wasn't giving the US expansion 100% of my attention. We were dipping our toes in. Finally, we realized a casual salesperson stationed in a beautiful resort town wasn't going to cut it. If we wanted to make a foothold in the US, we had to get really serious about the game, which meant we had to be prepared to spend some serious money—and make another big move. We had learned from our Ontario expansion that we could no longer "airplane" in from our West Coast head office. So we set up operations in the province. We came at it from the perspective that the restaurant was brand new to Ontarians, even though many people would have seen or been to a Boston Pizza if they visited any western provinces, including attending Expo '86. We weren't new; we were just new to *them*.

By the time we decided to enter the American market, Boston Pizza was just beginning to be part of the Canadian restaurant landscape. You could find one of our restaurants at busy suburban intersections in every western province, and at a few in Ontario. People knew the iconic BP sign, and that we also served ribs and salads. They were familiar with some of the more popular items on our menu, and knew some of our commercials by heart. They knew Boston Pizza to be a friendly, casual place where you could bring the whole family for a meal or catch the game with friends over pizza and beer.

But to Americans, we were nobodies. They knew nothing about us, our history or the Boston Pizza experience. But we were coming off a successful decade in Ontario. Our re-entry there was done right, and the Quebec expansion further proved we could adapt to suit different locales without eroding our core brand. These successes made me realize that we did indeed have something unique and with universal appeal. It wasn't just about the type of pizza we served, which is halfway between Chicago deep-dish and New York thin crust. The whole Boston Pizza experience seemed to translate across the country. Because each time we expanded, into Ontario, into Quebec and ultimately into the Atlantic provinces, people responded positively. They embraced us. It worked. Now I had to be willing to make yet another big move. But to where?

Before relocating to the US, I asked myself two questions: who is the competition, and where are they based? Turned out it was Dallas, Texas, a casual dining mecca with four times more restaurants per capita than New York City. And Dallas is headquarters to a lot of big players in the casual dining industry, including Chili's and Pizza Hut, which has offices in nearby Plano. Also it's an airline hub—you can fly from the Dallas/Fort Worth airport to any city in the US in under three hours. I had imagined my conversations with folks in the industry down in Dallas, them asking me how long I planned to stay there. I wanted to be able to tell them I lived there. It would be good for business. It would signal to potential franchisees and employees, suppliers, marketers and competitors that we're serious about the business of making it in the States.

Funny enough, Sandi and I had had one of our first dates in Dallas a couple years earlier, when I flew her in for a conference I was attending. I remember liking the city and the people, though I had never imagined living there. But in January 2001, she made a leap of faith and moved, along with her two children, Katie and Dan, to Dallas with me. Shortly after we unpacked, we held an intimate surprise wedding ceremony at our new home. It was another new beginning.

Soon after we had settled into our new house, I met a guy named Mike Best, a straight-shooting New Yorker who lived across the street. He had incredible retail experience and understood the American consumer. We really hit it off, so it wasn't long before I poached him to head up our US office.

By driving around Dallas I got my head around the scope of the market—and the huge task in front of us. Luckily, I love a challenge. But consider this: In the US, there are restaurant franchises that never become national brands. They remain regional and yet can have 300 to 400 stores. Ever heard of Pappadeaux Seafood Restaurant? Probably not. It's a chain of restaurants located primarily in Texas, New Mexico and Louisiana. In the same vein, big national restaurant companies like the one that owned Bennigan's can shut down hundreds of stores in one day. These are staggering numbers, involving millions of dollars. And here we were with about 150 stores in Canada at the time, hoping to penetrate this massive market.

At first it was daunting. I felt our size. I had to remind myself that Boston Pizza had taken 40 years to become the lion in the Canadian market. In the US, Boston's The Gourmet Pizza was still a cub. That's why I urge entrepreneurs to wait, to make sure they've completely tapped the Canadian market. When they're the lion in Canada, they stand a better chance of surviving down in the jungle of the US. I knew that several big, healthy companies, ones that do really well in Canada, didn't make it in the States. I also knew that a few popular American restaurant chains had never made inroads beyond the US border. But we had to start somewhere, and we had the experience, we had the right people and we had the right instincts to conquer that territory as well.

Another big hurdle at the time was the exchange rate. Back in the late 1990s, $100,000 Canadian was worth about $60,000 US. That's a big bite. I remember bringing a large cheque to a local Dallas bank. The money was meant for setting me up in the US. The cashier took one look at the amount, noted that it was in Canadian dollars and excused herself. She returned with her concerned-looking supervisor.

"Y'all realize that you're not going to get this much money when we deposit this, right?" The supervisor had never seen a Canadian cheque and didn't really know how to reconcile a 40% loss on the face value because of the exchange rate. But I had been prepared to spend more for everything we hoped to accomplish down there. George and I put our own money into the US expansion, not company money—upwards of $50 million over a decade.

That should give you a sense of our commitment to making the US expansion work.

You Can't Control Timing

Soon after we settled in Dallas, 9/11 happened. George and I were in Denver, Colorado, having attended the opening of the new stadium. We were checking out when we were informed that the airport was closed. We were speechless as we watched events unfold on the TV in our hotel room, where'd we ended up staying for a few more days while the planes remained grounded. After that, the whole country hunkered down. Doing business was already tough, with the tech bubble bursting and the country just starting to slip into a recession. Suddenly, if you weren't American, you were treated like an outsider. Investors were hard to find, franchisees even harder. Banks shut off the spigots. The US engaged in two very expensive wars, the effects of which you can feel in places like Killeen, Texas, where we have a franchise. It's home to a large army base, population 65,000, almost the size of the entire Canadian military. Every time 20,000 troops were deployed to the Middle East or Afghanistan, business dipped. When the soldiers returned, business boomed. You could chart it.

Along with those wars came the country-wide collapse of real estate, both commercial and residential, and then a seemingly endless recession. Expanding in the US during a recession seemed ill-advised. Far from bruising us, however, the recession helped us by settling down the market. Some of our biggest competitors, like Bennigan's, went under; others, including TGIF, Applebee's and Chili's, stopped their expansion plans. Wannabes and pretenders were kicked out of the market. Meanwhile, by growing slowly and more steadily, we've remained lean and strong. We've been doing our push-ups in the hallway, waiting for the giants-on-steroids to stumble. Today, we're properly financed. Our franchisees are financially sound. We are building at a manageable pace. We are again moving ahead. Remember, a place like Las Vegas wasn't built on winnings but on the backs of those people who lost their shirts. It's a harsh way to put it, but it's true.

So, 9/11, two wars and a big recession: those were big obstacles to a company hoping to expand in the States. Why proceed? Volume. The sheer potential for growth. The average successful store in Ontario can do $2.5 million a year. It's the same in the US—if you can break through. If you can compete, you'll grow fast, and you'll do some incredible numbers. And if you do well in the States, the world opens up to you. That's what attracts every entrepreneur, including those who come on *Dragons' Den,* those who say they're going to use Dragon investment money to break into the US market. The camera will often cut to my incredulous face. Many of these entrepreneurs know I'm the only Dragon who has attempted to expand into the US market with my company, indeed the only Dragon who actually lives in the States. Often, it's me they've come to convince because it's my expertise they seek. And they're stunned when I sometimes say "Wait." Get stronger. Grow bigger first. Because 9 times out of 10, they haven't finished tapping into the Canadian market. Then I tell them to have deep pockets.

Some listen to me, some don't. The problem is this: Entrepreneurs often see only dollar signs. They see the US as the promised land of customers. They see everyone there as a walking wallet. *The US is almost 10 times the population of Canada. I'll make 10 times the money. Even if I only corner 1% of the market!* Maybe. But what they completely forget is that they're also dealing with 10 times the competition. This makes for a very exciting and lucrative market but also one that's difficult and expensive to penetrate.

Even Small Decisions Have to Be Made Quickly

Americans love the casual dining experience, and the list of our competitors is formidable: TGIF, Applebee's, Chili's, California Pizza Kitchen, Buffalo Wild Wings, BJ's, and on and on. But if we're talking straight-up competition for a box of pizza, that list is epic: Papa John's, Domino's, Little Caesars and Pizza Hut, which will deliver a large pizza to your door for eight bucks. Because of their sheer size, those companies have millions of dollars to bombard radio and TV with loud commercials and deep discounts. So how do we compete with all that? We remind ourselves (and our franchisees) that Boston's The Gourmet Pizza is a premium pizza *restaurant*. And although we do deliver, we're about the dining experience, the service and the ambience.

By 2003, we had nine stores up and running. We could no longer see our American operation as an extension of our Canadian one. It had to stand alone. With that in mind, we trained our franchisees in the US, not Canada, and we used American suppliers only. And by treating our suppliers like partners, we were able to negotiate better prices. We tied their success in with ours.

Then came the tweaking, the million little decisions that had to be made in order to adjust Boston Pizza as it became Boston's The Gourmet Pizza. For instance, Perogy Pizza was not a big seller in the US, so we dumped it. Piling nachos on a metal plate and heating it up so the cheese melts doesn't fly in parts of the States. Americans tend to like individual nacho plates, so they can select their own ingredients. We also had to perfect our salsa and guacamole blends for the Southwest market in particular, because they were used to local Tex-Mex recipes. Then we added a beef dip sandwich to the menu. In the US, cheese isn't overseen by a marketing board like it is in Canada, so dairy is cheaper there. Same with chicken. Our US prices might be lower, but we make up for it in volume. Also, Americans don't take leisurely lunches. Enjoying a bottle of wine over a noontime pizza, as is common in our Quebec restaurants, is unheard of in Dallas, where diners have to be in and out in 35 minutes. Americans don't work harder than their Canadian counterparts, but they do have to drive more often to lunch destinations, so shaving off a couple minutes from the wait makes a huge difference. I know these things because that became my reality also. If I have time to take a lunch, it better be a fast meal and it better be convenient.

These decisions, these changes, have to be made quickly. Americans don't go back to restaurants that don't make their favourite foods exactly the way they like them. I have found that people who've never tried pizza come to love our pizza, and we can alter wings, nachos and sandwiches to suit different tastes because our core menu items are still pizza and pasta, our key brand. If someone were making these decisions in Canada, the entire process would be mired in meetings. That's the benefit of living in a country whose market we're trying to crack. I don't need a long discussion or a case study to understand that we should be breading our wings in the States. Doesn't matter why. That's the way Americans like their wings. Our research consists of asking *ourselves* what we think about our competitors' nachos or pizzas, or the guacamole or wings. Anyone working at Boston's is required to eat at other restaurants and report back. We better understand the American taste bud. Same with the dining experience. You'll see greeters at the door of a Boston's in the States—I've discovered Americans like that extra touch, and we're considering bringing it to our stores in other countries.

And then there's the look. We had to really stand out, so we decided to use the exterior of our store like a billboard, advertising that you can also have salads, pastas and ribs at Boston's The Gourmet Pizza. That's not just for the benefit of potential customers wondering what else we serve. I have to think of potential franchisees driving by who might be looking for another business to buy into. One of the best things going for us in the US is our novelty. We offer up something our competition has long run out of: new territory to conquer. If you're a successful franchisee selling fried chicken in Ohio, and you've saturated that state's market, you have to leave to expand your business. That's expensive. Boston's offers already successful franchisees with other companies an opportunity to stay in their state and expand their business with a new concept.

Most franchisees don't get into the business to open just one restaurant. They want to open several, and those are the kind of franchisees we love working with. For those who want to control entire territories, we give them first right of refusal. Ours is a tried-and-tested concept, with a long history of proven profits, and an interested franchisee knows he or she can quickly expand if successful with the first store, and we do what we can to encourage that. And although I did toy with the idea of starting in Texas and not expanding until we conquered that state first, our plan now is to grow regionally. By putting a Boston's in every state, we plan to establish a strong presence and grow around those stores. That's why, when you look at a map, we look scattershot, but beneath that seeming randomness there is a strategy.

Debt Tolerance Is Different Everywhere

Used to be it was much easier for American franchisees to secure financing than Canadian ones, especially in the early 2000s. Then we went through a real estate collapse that made banks question their practice of lending money so easily, many by breaking the law. Today, things are far more stable. But I've found that Americans generally have an easier relationship with debt. And even if Canadians wanted to carry more debt or take on a bigger mortgage, there are only a handful of major banks in Canada— whereas not long ago, anyone with a million dollars in assets could open a bank in the US. It's harder in Canada to take on more debt than you can afford. Not only is debt less frightening, it's easier to exaggerate your worth. I think of a woman who worked for me in operations. During a casual conversation a few years ago, she told me she'd just bought a house, same square footage as mine, swimming pool and all. I was baffled. We paid her well, but not *that* well. So I didn't know how she convinced a bank she could afford so much house. Further into the conversation she mentioned that she got an "excellent mortgage," 95%. The plan was to flip the property, she said. Turns out a lot of people across the country had the same plan. And it wasn't a very good one. When the economy dipped, it's no wonder so many Americans, with so little skin in the game, had no problem walking away from their mortgages and their homes. The recession made us more vigilant about picking potential franchisees. Today, even though the economy has stabilized, we spend a little more time looking into finances to make sure they hold up to scrutiny.

Americans Aren't Better at Business, but They Have to Be Faster

American business people are often accused of being brash. I don't agree with that. I think that because of the amount and the intensity of the competition in the States,

Americans act fast. They have to. Some people find it off-putting, but I love directness; I find it relaxing. Almost as much as I love making decisions, I love doing business with decision makers, people who don't need (or have) a whole lot of time to consider every angle and locate every obstacle. When your competition's breathing down your neck, you don't deliberate. You act. I learned how to speak that language in Canada, and I perfected it in Asia. Far from feeling overwhelmed by the challenges, I love that you'd better keep up or you'll be left in the dust. Business just isn't personal in the US. Emotions don't factor in when making decisions about money, a fact that dovetails with my rule that money decisions should be made rationally, with your head, not your heart or your gut. You can see why I had little trouble fitting in.

That said, when I moved to Dallas more than 10 years ago, I didn't know a soul. But far from it being a cold, unfriendly place, I've made some of my closest friends there, many who opened up the country to me. I think of Greg Osler, who I met on a plane. Sitting next to me, he noticed my Boston Pizza signet ring.

"Is that a championship ring of some kind?" he asked.

"Yes, from a championship company," I replied.

Turns out he owned a telephone company that had been trying to do business with Boston's. We chatted, and needless to say, he got the contract. Down here, meeting people and making contacts is an art form, and one of my favourite things about the country.

North-South Expansions Often Do Better Than East-West

In the US, we can't make decisions about future franchises based on the old model of analyzing a location's demographics and then planting a flag. Instead, we start with the franchisee. We find the right people with the right fit, and *then* we look at where *they* want to build. That's the only reason there's a Boston's in places like Shelby Township, Michigan—which, by the way, is our most successful franchise—or Rapid City, South Dakota. We had terrific franchisees who wanted to open up shop in these smaller cities. After we did the research and the due diligence, we gave them the go-ahead, and they're both doing gangbuster business. Not surprisingly, we have the most stores in Texas, a total of nine, proving that it's important to expand from the roots out.

Since living in the States, I've discovered an interesting pattern that will influence how we'll grow the company in the future. Franchises seem to do better when they expand along north-south lines—in long ovals—rather than stretching wide in an east-west pattern. The ovals tend to cover three zones; east, west and the middle. What works in Vancouver usually works in Seattle and Phoenix. What works in Manitoba seems to work down in Texas; the same goes for along the Ontario–New Jersey–Florida line. I think it's because people can migrate more easily in these directions: it's less unsettling when you relocate to remain in the same time zone. And people who share the same time zones seem to develop similar rhythms, tastes and appetites. It's not a scientific theory. It's just my observation.

As well, workers don't like to migrate east or west. If I have a problem staffing stores in South Dakota, I can't count on employees coming out from California or New York. I'm also finding that the American recession hit the East and West Coasts harder than the centre of the country, which saw less fluctuation in real estate values. But you can feel the economy bouncing back. Car manufacturers are back on their feet and making profits; banks are stricter but healthier and more reliable; and the real estate market, both residential and commercial, is starting to stabilize. All this makes it easier to find better and better franchisees. I've never been more optimistic about our future growth. After more than 10 years and tens of millions of dollars, we're finally getting traction in the States.

Every new decision made in the US expansion sprouted from our past experience. That's why, looking back, I can see that our initial expansions into Ontario and Asia weren't mistakes after all. We learned a lot. And those lessons are paying off today as we open our 48th restaurant in the US. Because here's the thing I've come to understand the most: you have to make it in the US if you want to make an impact beyond North America. My moving to the States has secured the future growth of our company, and it has also opened my eyes to a more interesting market, one that might prove to outperform the US in ways I never imagined: Mexico.

Grow Where There Are More Jobs, Not Just More People
Last year for insurance purposes I had to get a physical. The company sent a nurse to my home in Dallas to take

and test some blood. She was a little woman who couldn't have weighed more than 90 pounds wet.

"Where you from?" she asked as I rolled up my sleeve. She had a slight Spanish accent, one you hear everywhere in Texas. "You don't sound like you're from here."

"Canada," I said. "Little town in Manitoba."

"Manitoba? Where's that?"

"It's a province in the middle of Canada. There are 10 provinces and 3 territories in Canada," I said, probably sounding like a bossy schoolteacher.

"Oh yeah? I never knew that. But you probably don't know how many states there are where I'm from."

"Fifty," I said, assuming she was talking about the States.

"No. I'm from Mexico."

She had me there. I had no idea how many states are in Mexico.

"And you probably couldn't name them, either," she added.

She had me again. She wasn't being mean. It was all very matter-of-fact. There I was judging her geographical ignorance about Canada when I was just as guilty, maybe even more so given that our fourth Mexican location was under construction in Villahermosa, and we were meeting soon in Mexico City with a large investment group interested in expanding across the country.

Why are we doing so well in Mexico? The economy there is on fire, with big growth in the middle- to upper-income brackets. Only roughly 15% of the Mexican population can afford to eat out, but that 15% spends a lot of money.

They want to experience what Americans freely enjoy. Our restaurant–sports bar concept makes total sense to Mexicans. Different sports are shown on the TVs—you're more likely to catch the soccer game than hockey. But the family-friendly atmosphere is the real draw. And I don't say that lightly. Our franchisees explained why we had to redesign the layout of our Mexican dining areas to accommodate larger tables for the Sunday rush. It's a tradition in Mexico to eat with family every Sunday, so we had to be able to seat 10, 20, 30 people at the same time. These are cultural changes; they're more subtle than a tweak to a recipe. We learned that lesson in Quebec, where singing and good wine at lunch are all part of the Boston Pizza experience.

Today, if you go to one of the two Boston's in Mérida, you wouldn't be able to tell the difference between a busy night there and one in Oakville. Our franchisees in Mexico have done an incredible job of replicating the experience. If the local sign maker couldn't design the BP logo to look exactly the way it looks in Canada, they imported it. If an ingredient wasn't available to achieve the exact same recipe, they imported that as well. We import our bread to Mexico because they can't make it the same way there. Mexicans don't want a Mexican version of Boston's bread. They want Boston's.

In Mexico, surprisingly enough, there is no casual dining chain that competes with us directly. In Mexico, a sports bar and restaurant franchise—never mind one that serves gourmet pizza with premium toppings—is considered a novelty. In fact, in the cities that we're in right now—Mérida, Ciudad del Carmen and Villahermosa—we're often considered a fine dining establishment. And we do steady business because we didn't make the mistake of opening up in tourist towns, whose fortunes rise and fall dramatically, depending on how that industry's doing. And those cities are also plagued by drug trafficking, and the violence and instability that go along with it. I like to build in cities with a strong local economy, with a good-sized population of working-class people with factory, oil or mining jobs, who make a decent salary and can afford to go out for dinner now and again. That's how we built out in Canada. Boston Pizza came of age in places like Prince George and Fort McMurray, where a strong local economy supported our business. We're using that model to expand in Mexico.

Since the day that nurse came to my house, I've brushed up on my Mexican geography and politics. There's no excuse for me not to know as much as I can about that country, since it's looking like the Mexican market might be more lucrative for us than the US. In fact, we recently signed agreements to open another 8 stores, including ones in Mexico City. And we have a potential partner on board that could mean 300 more stores within the next decade.

Our success in Mexico has given us the confidence to start eyeing Brazil and Colombia, two countries with an emerging middle class that isn't going to tolerate anything that keeps international business opportunities away. They're changing in the right ways, and I expect to see franchises operating in those and other countries within the next decade.

Exciting times. Mexico proved to us that our concept works. The idea of a family-oriented pizza restaurant and sports bar makes sense to someone in Shelby Township, Michigan, and in Mérida, Yucatán. The menu might be in Spanish, but the experience is the same.

Bottom line is, if I didn't think that we do it better than anyone else, I wouldn't get out of bed in the morning. When we're given the opportunity to compete, more often than not, we win. I like those odds. Oh, and more good news: I fully expect to have, after we overcome some paperwork hurdles, our first Boston's franchise open in Boston by the time this book is on the shelves.

Solid Business Models Are Transferable

When I was a young police officer, there were some really tough bars in Prince George, especially the Canada Hotel. You never knew what to expect when you walked through its doors. Someone could come up from behind and crack a bottle over your head, or knife you on the way to the washroom. Or they might pull up a stool and give you a warm hug. People who frequented those places were unpredictable, unknowable and mostly unconcerned about consequences. So you went in prepared. Mostly, you went in as a team. In my years on the force, I was always partnered with tough, instinctual guys. I was lucky: I know what it feels like to walk into an uncertain situation with someone having your back. When you have that, you can keep your senses focused on the things they need to be alert to, knowing you'll be able to react. You can have confidence in the face of fear.

Now when I contemplate a risk or a tough decision, I think to myself, *You know how to do this. Fear isn't going anywhere, so take action anyway. And if anything goes wrong, someone you trust has your back.* With that attitude, I can accomplish anything. I make confident decisions because I know I can recalculate when necessary. Not *if* necessary, *when* necessary—because if I've learned anything with our expansion into the US and Mexico, it's this: things change. My job now is to make another decision in the face of change. And to put people in place who can take this company into the next generation. George and I aren't going to be around forever, but expanding our operations has taught us to think generationally, not just into the next decade. We want our companies to be around for a hundred years and beyond. To do that, we have to continue to grow at a strong and steady pace, solidify the base as we go and continue to employ a decision-making process that has served us well.

Shortly after I moved to the States, George and I were faced with yet another big decision. We had finally bought out Dave Gillespie and Bud Grant. Boston Pizza ended up being an incredible investment for them, but now George and I each owned 50% of a very lucrative enterprise. The company was profitable, stable and growing, so we wanted to find a way to distribute the wealth. We weren't interested in selling. First of all, we didn't want to place our beloved company in anyone else's hands. And second, it would signal retirement for both of us, and neither of us was interested in that or ready for it. We have so much more work to do and so many new territories to conquer. It's just becoming interesting again.

We also looked into selling part of the company by issuing shares to the public. But although sharing ownership wasn't unappealing, sharing control was. Luckily, at the time, there was a third option in Canada: setting up an income trust. That's what we decided to do. We called it the Boston Pizza Royalties Income Fund, and what we've essentially done is sell the Boston Pizza International trademark to the fund, which in turn licenses it back to Boston Pizza International for 99 years. It sounds like a complicated financial food chain. But simply put, we receive 7% from our franchisees. We take 4% of that and put it into the royalties fund. This has enabled us to keep the company we love in our hands, reward investors and share some of the wealth in an incentive program with employees.

But just when I thought I could relax a bit and cut back on the workload, another opportunity dropped into our laps: buying into Mr. Lube. George met Ted Ticknor at a Young Presidents' Organization meeting, they started to spend time on the golf course, and we soon all became fast friends. A Prairie boy like me, Ted helmed Mr. Lube, a successful chain of oil-change retailers across Canada. Our initial conversations were about the income trust, and how Mr. Lube could either set one up itself or get into ours. We decided against it. Oil change shops and restaurants are just too different. Ted loved how we ran our company, though, and wanted us to join him in his. He offered us a great opportunity: 25% ownership and 50% control over decisions, the latter of which was more important to us than equity. We'd no doubt make a profit, but we learned the hard way that, to feel comfortable, we needed to have crucial control over the decision-making process. We set the paperwork in motion for this new partnership.

Then Ted started getting horrible backaches. He'd stretch on the fairway, complaining about a sharp pain in his lower back. Golf looks deceptively passive, but it can take its toll on the body, like any sport. So we chalked it up to age and didn't think too much about it.

Turned out to be advanced prostate cancer. By the time they found it, the doctors couldn't do anything for him. Ted was a vital man, a wealthy man, a man who could buy the best treatment available, but he was delivered the worst possible news anyone could receive. I felt gut-punched. Sandi and I visited him on his deathbed. I asked if there was anything we could do for him. He stretched out his weak arms. All he wanted from me was a hug.

Ted handed us an incredibly opportunity, so we owed Ted a healthy company. George and I decided to do for Mr. Lube what we did when we bought Boston Pizza: turn the company into a pure franchising model, with a couple of corporate stores used only for training and testing. We met with the shareholders and explained our vision. There was resistance, naturally. But we hired some tough managers, who went about standardizing practices, setting up conventions and cleaning up operations. With the company on stronger footing, we began to sell off all the corporate stores. Some Mr. Lube managers got financing and bought their stores. Some were Boston Pizza franchisees. Oil and pizza didn't compete with each other, so that wasn't a problem. And because we had such a solid franchise model and understand the ins and outs of licensing, we realized it doesn't really matter what we're selling—oil, pizza or hockey tickets—a solid business is a solid business. And we knew from experience that this model worked.

Today, Mr. Lube is a pure franchise organization, and we just closed a deal that will put a Mr. Lube in every Walmart across Canada over the next few years. This is a story of a good business opportunity that came on the heels of a great tragedy, but it also proves further that my story is really just a giant network of introductions and relationships.

Say Yes to What You Fear Most

No sooner had the Mr. Lube deal closed than I received a strange call from a confident woman who worked at the CBC in Toronto. Her name was Tracie Tighe and she was producer on a show called *Venture,* which I caught from time to time. She wondered if George and I wanted to take part in a segment called "The Big Switcheroo," in which managers and employees take on the challenge of each other's jobs. I wasn't completely convinced that I should go on camera, but I said sure, come on out, we'll talk about it. I have to admit, the filming process was fun.

And although I didn't think I was going to be the next George Clooney, I did get a real kick out of those days in front of the camera, and our employees had a lot of fun too. And then I put it away.

Fast-forward a month later, and this same woman called me again, this time offering me another shot on TV. But it sounded a little more involved than just a couple of days spent with a cameraman following us around. The producers wanted to fly to Vancouver to audition George and me, and a bunch of other wealthy people—some we knew, some we didn't—for a show the CBC was producing called *Dragons' Den.* The program was already being broadcast on the BBC, so it was sort of like a franchise. George bowed out right away, saying TV was not his thing. The *Venture* shoot had been fun, but I was a little uncomfortable watching myself later, and besides, what the hell business did I have being on a TV every week? So I wasn't much interested, either.

Then Tracie tried appealing to the nationalistic side of Boston Pizza, saying it was a home-grown success story and this program, *Dragons' Den,* would be a great way to give a face to a big Canadian company. (She would have been a good Expo '86 organizer.) She persuaded me to sit in on the auditions. What harm was there in that?

It was a Sunday, 8 a.m. I put on a suit and tie, and gave it my best shot. Pitchers were brought out, just like you see today on the show, and one by one, the others auditioning and I interrogated, laughed, sampled and probed. It was a lot of fun, and it felt very natural. The thing is, entrepreneurs just love to talk about business, whether cameras are rolling or not. I get asked this a lot about *Dragons' Den:* Is any of it scripted? And the answer is absolutely not. That passion's just there, with all of us.

A few days later, I was offered a spot on the new show. But the idea of doing what I did during the auditions for real, and for longer? I just couldn't imagine pulling it off on national TV. I said no. Tracie was disappointed and said she'd give me a few days to think about it.

Later that night I told Sandi I turned down the offer.

"You did what?"

"Yeah, I said no. I don't want to be on TV."

"Jim," she said, "do you have any idea what this kind of publicity would do for the business?" She reminded me that, although there were dozens of Boston Pizzas in Ontario, we'd only begun to spread to the East Coast. And we'd just bought into Mr. Lube. Surely, it couldn't hurt.

"It's the CBC, Jim. I think you should do it. This could be a great opportunity for you and the company. Not to mention fun."

We watched the British version on DVD and, I have to confess, I was riveted. But I kept coming back to the same question: I loved talking business and grilling people about opportunities, but would viewers care about business at that level? In the end, it didn't matter. Throw a business idea in front of me and I can talk about it for hours. If no one watched, that was for the broadcaster to worry about.

I changed my mind. I decided to give it a shot. Why? Because Sandi was right: no matter what, it would be good publicity for the business. And I trust Sandi. She wants what's best for me and for the business. Plus it'd be a lark, and it had been a long time since I'd taken a flyer on something.

You Can't Fake Enthusiasm

That first shoot for season one had all the hallmarks of a start-up. We all had a ton of enthusiasm, but no idea what to expect. The pitchers and the Dragons were equal parts nervous and excited. We each had different motives for wanting the show to work, but there was a shared sense that we were in it together. Naturally, the first few pitches the producers threw out at us were ringers, just meant to loosen us up and entertain us. Some businesses were so small, they were barely a fart in a windstorm—and I said so. But when the yelling began and the tears started to flow, I realized that there were stakes involved, that these were real entrepreneurs. Ever the police officer, I leaned over towards the other Dragons and told them we had to smarten up and get serious. No more goofing around, I said. There was real money on the table, so let's give them some real feedback.

None of us had any idea how successful the show would go on to become. And we certainly didn't have any idea that Canadians would be as fascinated and inspired by the world of entrepreneurship as they've been. But seven seasons in we're still pulling in the top TV ratings in the country, and still introducing Canadians to new product ideas and businesses. And I've made what I believe are lifelong friends. Being on the show together, we've gone through some things. We've developed the same kind of esprit de corps I experienced with my troop mates during RCMP training. We may disagree with each other on *Dragons' Den*—hell, we always disagree with each other, that's the nature of the show—but we leave any animosity we've displayed on the set. We don't disrespect each other in public, we don't tell tales about each other to the press. We don't undermine each other's decisions because we don't assume we know what goes into making them. We trust each other. We have each other's backs. You can watch us fight on TV over businesses, insult each other and guard our interests. Behind the scenes, we are a unified team. I would consider the other Dragons some of my closest friends, for whom I'd do anything.

Dragons' Den has also become a great launching pad for new products, many making their debut on the show. No Dragon had ever pounced faster on a new product than I did during season five. Brian and Corin Mullins of Sechelt, BC, had developed a cereal blend called Holy Crap, a mix of chia seeds, hemp and dried fruit, that I knew had terrific health benefits, including increasing regularity (hence the clever name, which I loved). As a food guy, I pride myself in keeping up with trends. And I knew that chia seeds were a quickly emerging "superfood" that was being tested in breads, pastas and pizza dough. I was all over it, and we did a handshake deal in a record-breaking eight minutes. The producers told me they had to cut a minute or two off the top and bottom of the raw footage, but the segment ran pretty much as is—also a first. Pitches during the shoot tend to run at least a half an hour, sometimes as long as one and a half hours. But you see only about eight minutes of any given pitch on air.

But in the due diligence process, as happens often, the Holy Crap deal slowly began to fall apart. The Mullinses had experienced a massive uptick in sales when the pitch aired. Now they didn't want to give as much of the company away, naturally, and weren't as keen on changing some of their procedures to what I had hoped. These are good things to understand about each other. And in the end, we discovered we were not a great match. Our visions for the company didn't line up. I wished them the best and we moved on.

But here's the spectacular thing about the deal. When the pitched aired, it caused an incredible sensation. Sometimes success goes beyond a great product. Holy Crap, with its chia seeds, was launched into a marketplace ripe for new superfoods, and this stuff tastes great. Online orders went from 10 bags a day to 10 per minute. Yearly sales went from $50,000 to $2 million. That's all terrific, and almost to be expected when you're dealing with a national show that sometimes gets as many as two million viewers a week. The popularity of Holy Crap meant that the local post office had to hire two new full-time employees to keep up with the ongoing demand. Local lawyers, accountants and business consultants were all hired during the due diligence process and beyond to help the Mullinses deal with a rapidly growing business in a small island community. They've gone on to build a distribution facility in nearby Gibsons, with plans to build a plant in Brockville, Ontario. Even though I'm not a partner, I'm nothing but thrilled for them. That one pitch has changed not only the Mullinses' fortunes but those of many people around them.

There was a happier ending for me with the Frogbox pitch in season six. And it was all about Doug Burgoyne. That guy hit me at the gut level right away. His terrific reusable moving box idea had already caught on enough for Doug to begin franchising in the west. Of course, this perked me up, but my decision to invest was based less on the business idea and the bit of money Doug was already bringing in and more on him. In my gut I knew he had the winning qualities to close the deal.

Right from the beginning he impressed all of us, including George, who is my silent partner in all my *Dragons' Den* deals. Doug showed up at our first meeting with all of his paperwork in order—a big deal given that we were looking at 30 deals from that season. So Doug was keen from the get-go; you could tick off that doubt. Then we got a good look at his accounting and finances. His projections were sound, and he wasn't carrying a lot of debt. Everything he said about the company was true. And his claims passed muster with my accountants.

Since moving from handshake to partner, Doug has kept us informed at every stage of his company's growth, just like George and I did with Dave and Bud. The first thing Doug wanted to do was head to the States and start conquering the American market. It's an inclination just about every Canadian entrepreneur has. We were able to persuade Doug to hold off, to build out in Canada first, and with the attention from *Dragons' Den*, that meant potential franchisees began contacting him. But since then, we've helped Doug open his first of many American franchises in Boise, Idaho.

You may also remember Evergreen Memories, a small business pitched by Margot Woodward of Dryden, Ontario. The company grows tree seedlings for giveaway gifts at weddings and corporate events. I liked everything about the business; it's eco-friendly and unique, but what appealed to me most was that Margot was already closing on big clients like Molson and Jamieson Vitamins, which were repeat customers. She had momentum and vision, and her company was already showing a profit. And when she talked about growing tree seedlings in California to cut down on shipping costs to the States, I could see a way to do the deal.

What I liked about both Doug and Margot is that they had already made several crucial decisions that set their companies in the right direction, decisions we discovered in due diligence to be sound. That's what due diligence really boils down to. The black-and-white numbers tell you only part of the story about the company you're potentially going to invest in, let alone the entrepreneurs. What you're really looking at in the due diligence process is their pattern of decision making. Have they steered the company wrong? If so, how did they correct that? Do they have the right people in place today? Do they solve problems productively? Are they reactive or decisive? Will they take outside direction? Are they open to changes, minor or major? All of that information is more important to me than knowing they have a healthy bottom line. I want to know what kinds of decisions the entrepreneur makes.

Another deal I sealed from *Dragons' Den* was with a family in Maple Ridge, BC, pitching Easy Daysies, a magnetic calendar to keep kids on schedule. Elaine Comeau came up with the idea at her kitchen table, from where she was still assembling and shipping the product when she pitched it on the show. They hadn't made much money, but the income was growing steadily. Mostly, Elaine made a powerful impression on all five Dragons. She's one of those rare people who are born entrepreneurs. She had a clear sense of how to move the product forward and where it could grow. Her early decisions were all smart. She kept the idea simple. It remained a small home business for as long as she could handle it. She didn't quit her day job as a teacher, so she hadn't taken unnecessary risks with her family's money or their future.

She was someone you could reason with, and she handled the pressure of the Den with a lot of grace. What she showed was consistency of character: she was the same in the Den as she was across the boardroom table. That's not a small thing. I've been wowed by a lot of pitchers on the program, only to be disappointed by how they present themselves in the boardroom. With Elaine, I got a good gut feeling about her right away. Plus she's a source of incredible enthusiasm, and I always feel enlivened after a meeting with her and her family. I mean, she's got me really interested in magnets!

Your First Decision Isn't Always Your Best Decision

Saying yes to *Dragons' Den* was one of the single best decisions I've ever made—with the help of my wife, Sandi, of course, who knew me well enough to question my first decision of saying no. She helped me change my mind. I also had a mental image of what someone on TV should look like, and it wasn't a 65-year-old man. This was an old idea. I had worked only briefly with Tracie on the *Venture* shoot, and while it was fun, it wasn't enough time to get to that place where you know you can truly trust someone. And I wasn't just a business executive. If I became a Dragon, I would be the public face of Boston Pizza and Mr. Lube. What if I said or did something that would reflect badly on those companies? These were valid concerns, ones that churned through my well-oiled decision-making machine. And the answer to TV kept coming out as "no." I'm grateful that Sandi helped change my mind.

Deciding to become a Dragon has had an incredibly positive impact on my business. The great publicity has contributed, I think, to Boston Pizza being one of the few casual dining chains that didn't really suffer through the recent recession. In fact, it grew. Also, thanks to *Dragons' Den* I've gotten involved in some fantastic businesses. Another, less obvious, result of the program, and one I'm most proud of, is the so-called Dragons' Den Effect. The BBC employed the label first, using a term coined by the chief of the UK Intellectual Property Office after noticing a dramatic rise in patent applications since the show debuted there in 2005. The CBC sent around an article documenting this phenomenon, including stats that show the same steady rise in patent applications in Canada since the program began airing here in 2006. As well, contestants on the Den often see a big jump in sales and attention.

I'm a franchisor. I get a thrill from helping people make a successful go at something, especially if I've had a hand in creating the venture. I get that same thrill when I hear about the benefits others have enjoyed because of the success of the program. Even the ones who got away. *Dragons' Den* is an interesting place for me to hone my decision-making method, particularly when it comes to that crucial separation of head, heart and gut. I may love a product in the Den, as I did Holy Crap, and be impressed with the potential to make money. But the Mullinses saw the direction of their company very differently from how I did. My gut told me that was a recipe for future trouble. You have to walk away from those deals, no matter how lucrative they may be. And when I walk away under those circumstances, I never look back. I never second-guess those decisions. They're always the right ones.

On *Dragons' Den* I work very closely with Rowan Anders, a young investment analyst who waits backstage after I've made a deal. His job is to get the ball rolling on due diligence as soon as possible, after that on-air handshake. From the green room he watches all the pitches unedited as they're happening. He's become pretty adept at reading me. He knows exactly when I'm about to make a decision to invest. He says I get quiet. He notices that I tune out the other Dragons; I lean ever so slightly away from them, to pay better attention to the pitcher. And he can tell when I'm listening to my head, heart or gut when it comes to a pitch. The easiest one to recognize is my gut. Rowan says that, when I like someone, I lean in, elbows on knees, responding positively to the person's energy. I lean away, cover my mouth and cross my legs, apparently, when I don't like the pitcher. It's automatic: I don't notice I'm doing it.

With Frogbox, my body language said right away that I was "in." The business was so new that I wasn't making the decision to invest with my head. Yet, Doug Burgoyne made such a solid impression on me, he was so full of enthusiasm, that I was practically rolling up my sleeves, ready to dig into the paperwork. In my gut I knew Doug was the kind of entrepreneur who could make anything work if he believed in it. Same with Evergreen Memories. I just knew that Margot could make something that innovative and tricky (shipping live plants) work, and that she would only grow her business. Neither of these entrepreneurs needed me to come in and fix their early decisions. What they both needed was some money and a bit of guidance to keep building on the momentum they'd already generated by having made such smart decisions to begin with. To me, that's an ideal partnership.

But besides having made some potentially lucrative investments, there's another reason, a bigger reason, I'm glad I made the decision to become a Dragon. Across the country, at the elementary, high school and postsecondary levels, schools are using the *Dragons' Den* pitch model to teach students how to value a business, how to pitch the idea for funding and how to create a business plan. I get a lot of invitations to speak at schools. I remember one visit to a high school in downtown Toronto. I had buttonholed Kevin O'Leary to come with me. You could have heard a pin drop when we hit the stage. The auditorium was packed, kids practically hanging from the rafters. After our presentation they all wanted to talk about entrepreneurship in Canada. They wanted to know what kind of businesses make it and what kind don't. They wanted to know what one needs to succeed, and what kind of education or experience was vital.

I can still picture their faces. I remember thinking, if *Dragons' Den* has had anything to do with inspiring these kids to become entrepreneurs, I am proud as hell to be a small part of that spark. Maybe some of them will finish high school, go on to do an MBA or land a corporate job. Maybe others will discover something they're passionate about and start their own businesses, ones that create job opportunities or economic growth in their communities. Who knows?

Funding successful ideas, and making money with savvy entrepreneurs, is the essence of venture capitalism. It's what *Dragons' Den* is all about. But inspiring these students, showing them that if we can do it, so can they—well, there's no greater feeling on the planet. All this I get to experience because I changed my mind and decided to say yes to leaving my comfort zone and becoming a Dragon. I also proved to myself that at age 65, I was still able to take a big leap into the unknown and try something pretty terrifying, with no guarantee that it would pay off. And paid off it has. Not financially, not yet. It's too soon in the business cycle to tell if any of my *Dragons' Den* investments will earn out. But you can't put a price on helping to ignite the entrepreneurial spirit in this country's kids. It's an incredible feeling.

Another Thing That Improves with Age: Decision Making

In 2011, this unlikely TV star was approached by the producers of *Dragons' Den* to participate, along with Arlene Dickinson, in a series called *The Big Decision*. I was already knee-deep in writing this book about making decisions, so it felt like fate. It also sounded like an interesting concept: each episode would feature one of us analyzing two companies facing big challenges. Then we were to decide whether to invest in one of the companies, both of them or neither. Our money would help turn things around for them, and it would be a bargain investment for us. It was during the filming of the show that I really started to notice, for the first time, the pattern of my decision-making process: emotional about work, rational when it comes to money and instinctual about people.

Dragons' Den is a very different television animal from *The Big Decision.* In the Den, entrepreneurs come to us in their shiny best. They bring the best possible versions of themselves, their product, their pitch and their projections. We don't know if we made the right decision to invest in them until *after* the show. That's when we get to test their product, examine their books and visit their operations. *The Big Decision* is the opposite. I visit the companies' operations and look at their books first and *then* decide whether to invest. In many ways, it's more like the real world of venture capitalism than *Dragons' Den*.

One of the companies I was asked to assess was a bolt-and-fastener factory based in my home province of Manitoba. The plan: put on my "ice face" and visit the plant, without giving away my investment intentions. It's a TV show, after all, and we needed some mystery. Problem was, I knew before I even got out of the car that the company was in big trouble. Ten feet inside the front door, I knew it would be out of business before the show aired. I didn't need 40 years in business to figure that out. The waist-high weeds in the parking lot were the first dead giveaway. The cluttered entryway was the second. Worse, communication had broken down between the employees and owners. No one spoke to each other in the hallways.

It was hard for me to fake any kind of enthusiasm for the cameras. My eyes darted around the dusty, dirty plant. Nobody who worked there would make eye contact with me. I knew from my time as a police officer that that's a dead giveaway something's wrong. The owners had invited me there to help, but employees were being evasive.

What else? No one seemed to really be in charge, and the company's chief competition was in China, where productivity and efficiency are just the price of entry when it comes to business. Then we looked at the company's finances, and I had a flashback to my early days in business in Penticton. I knew what it was like to have poor financial discipline. I knew how it felt to be generating sales, to be actually making money but earning none of it. It's confusing to the point of being traumatic.

The producers were hoping that, being from Manitoba, I'd have a soft spot for a homespun business. But my gut told me that the employees would have a difficult time changing. You could tell that any enthusiasm for the work had long exited the building. No one wanted to be there. And once that attitude settles in, you can't get rid of it. I told the producers that the factory would be shuttered before the show went to air, and sadly, I was right.

We also visited a wooden fence company in New Brunswick that made a great product and had once brought in big bucks from the US market. By 2009, however, profits went south along with the American economy. I liked the family running the business a lot, and I liked the product they made. But I had a gut sense that they wouldn't do the one thing required: get financial discipline in the form of a chief financial officer (or CFO). You may think that the last decision a struggling company should make is to hire an expensive employee. But a CFO would have provided an accurate assessment of the company's financial situation and signalled to its competitors that it was, indeed, a multi-million-dollar enterprise. A CFO would also have brought much-needed financial discipline to the bottom line. I tried to find a way, but in the end I couldn't invest. Thankfully, the company did secure a big client and made a large sale that pulled it back from the brink and turned things around.

Two companies really impressed me, though, and I made the decision to back both. One was a beer company out of BC's Fraser Valley. I loved its uniqueness; it had great flavours. But a few bad batches and some shoddy bookkeeping almost did it in. I offered to back the company so it could upgrade its equipment, put together a tight business plan and throw muscle into marketing to try to move more beer. Plus I connected to this family-run business. I also threw my support behind an Ontario company that made ice wine. The owners had two things going for them: willingness to change and a great product. And I liked them a lot too. They needed financial discipline and a strong partner; I could supply both. In the end, though, it always boils down to due diligence, and as I write this, we are still working on closing those two deals.

Checklist for Decisions about Risk and Change

My RCMP training taught me the most crucial business lesson there is: Always do something. That's the one thing that sets successful people apart from not-so-successful people—the ability to actually *make* a decision. Unsuccessful people freeze in the face of choice. Why does this happen? It's fear of the unknown that keeps us stuck. Or fear of making the wrong decision. Sometimes it's easier to continue doing things the old, familiar way, even if that way is all wrong. But a big change will take you to a whole new place in business, and in life. And I have found that I can often make better decisions from that new vantage point. Here are a few things to keep in mind when you hit choppy waters—and you will hit them:

1. Get Over Your Fear. When companies grow, it can be a time of fear. Fear stops progress and kills momentum. I've seen fear put police officers in dire situations, and I've seen it undermine good businesses and the people who run them. I've also seen smart, experienced people who've made a bad initial decision and then course-correct and get unstuck. Do I wait until fear subsides until I make a decision? Never. I make decisions despite any fear. And *then* the fear subsides. That's how it works.

2. Reward Loyalty. In business, tough times show you who's got your back. You might be sweating it out in a downswing, but you do get to see what your partners and colleagues are made of. So whenever I get angry about a franchisee who steps out of line, I try to determine if it's a loyalty issue, and if it is, I try to remedy that. The key to expansion today is having the right partners on the ground to help us find and train franchisees and form a strong partnership with them. Perhaps a like-minded company that wants to grow right alongside Boston Pizza. Having that common goal will help build loyalty.

3. The Only Thing You Can Control Is Your Attitude. My early business's financial situation in Penticton and the Vancouver weather during Expo '86 taught me that, in times of crisis, the best thing to do is show up. At Expo there was no use matching doom with gloom; besides, weather was something I couldn't control. So I tried to set the tone every morning. I didn't stay away, didn't take the back way in. Instead, I brought as much enthusiasm as I could with me. I'm not talking about whistling in graveyards. I'm talking about not allowing negativity to infiltrate. Negativity is corrosive. It eats away at progress. And hiding and avoiding are never options.

4. Remain Entrepreneurial. I've mentioned this a lot, that during our worst crises, like Expo '86, we stayed flexible and innovative, changing prices and policies to match the moment. And we made those changes immediately. A lot of companies claim they're entrepreneurial, but every decision they make is dragged through the corporation's process, which requires paperwork and meetings to finalize the execution. I don't like a lot of meetings. Most aren't necessary. I like to make a decision with my heart, head or gut, whichever feels right, and then act on it. Often a good idea will come to me if I just take it easy.

5. You Can't Repair Bad Word of Mouth. The focus at Boston Pizza has always been a great guest experience. Restaurants are a big part of what people talk about—it's all about weather, sports, TV, movies, traffic . . . and food. Bad word of mouth will kill you faster than a cockroach in the kitchen. This influences all our decisions. Even after our retreat from there, we knew Asia and Ontario were money-making territories. But our gut also told us that if we continued to operate in either area without the proper people on the ground, the restaurants would flounder and we'd taint the Boston Pizza brand across the board, and probably for good. We'd become associated with poor service and inconsistency, which is death to a franchise. Shutting down in both territories was a preventative measure, and a smart decision, even though it was a tough one.

EPILOGUE

"Anyone who stops learning is old, whether at twenty or eighty. Anyone who keeps learning is young."
—Henry Ford

It's Never Too Later to Become a Better Decision Maker
The body doesn't lie. If you're older than 50, you know what I mean. I've got better at listening to it; I eat better, I get more exercise. I'm in great shape for someone past retirement age, but I don't take my health for granted. And although I may not be able to chase a suspect down a dark, cold alley (well, I might not be able to catch them), my decision-making skills have never been sharper. Head, heart and gut, those three areas still tackle very different problems, but my formula hasn't failed me. I continue to hone this method in ways that have come to work for me. Even while playing golf.

Golf figures large in my story. I love it for all the obvious reasons. First, you're outside. There is no better tonic than spending a half a day with good friends, enjoying cold drinks, in fine weather. And walking is the perfect exercise. Plus I've made some great deals on the golf course, and made some good connections—getting to know Ted Ticknor of Mr. Lube being one of the most important ones. But for the longest time I thought golf was a waste of four hours. I remember seeing these sunburned guys come into Boston Pizza in Penticton. I was grateful for their business, especially when it was quiet in the restaurant, but I didn't understand the game's draw. Yet everyone I knew played, so I had to see what I was missing out on. But when I finally took up the game at the ripe old age of 47, I was lousy. I mean, I was a *bad* golfer. This baffled me because I was good at sports, from baseball to hockey to football. I was in good shape, and I have excellent eye-hand coordination. Plus I was keen to learn. But, to put it simply, I was terrible at golf.

Why? Because I thought golf was about physical skill. That all you had to do was walk up to the green, stick a tee in the ground, grab a club and take a whack at the ball with some degree of accuracy and strength. I thought all you needed was a good arm and great aim, and that the only goal in golf was to get the ball as close as possible to the hole. On the surface of it, that's not totally inaccurate: you do need muscle and aim to land a ball. But I had never been taught to use other parts of my body when playing golf—my heart, my head and my gut. I didn't know about the million little variances and subtleties that went into deciding how to approach this particular golf ball, under these particular circumstances, on this particular green, on that particular day. I didn't know that landing a hole-in-one is less a game of skill than it is the outcome of a series of good decisions (and luck!). But once I figured that out, I fell in love with the game, the same way I fell in love with business. They're the same, after all: a good golf game and a successful business are each the result of a series of solid decisions.

Now, long before I take a swing at the ball, I take into consideration a number of things: What time are we playing? Where are we playing? What's my body doing these days? How are my knees? My shoulders? My elbows and wrists? Who am I playing with? How's their body doing? What's the weather going to be like? What should I wear? Which shoes? Are we walking or riding around the course? I think about these things before I even get there.

Then I approach the hole. The marker says 150 yards to the teeing area. But I haven't taken into consideration yet the direction of the wind, the hills, the bunkers, the condition of the grass or whether I'll be facing into the sun. All of this information will help me to make my decision about which club to use, and much depends on the club. It will determine how close I get the ball to the hole. I start by eliminating clubs. I know I'm not going to use the putter. I'm also not going to use my three or five wood. I usually pick a seven iron for 150 yards. If I made the wrong decision, I'll make adjustments at the next hole. I want to win, but I can only do it one hole at a time.

Mostly, I've discovered that playing golf is the best way

to get to know and understand people, from partners to prospective clients to investors. I do a lot of my business on the golf course, and because I do business in several cities and countries, I belong to a lot of golf clubs. And I'll let you in on a little secret: It's not about the golf. It's all about the connections.

An average game is four hours, and four hours is often just enough time to spend with someone to enable you to make informed decisions about them, to get a real gut sense about the kind of person they are. And it's not through a long conversation. Words tell me next to nothing about a person. Watching how the person plays golf gives me an intimate look at how they make decisions. That's what I need to know. Not where they went to school, or how their kids are doing, or what they think of the current administration. Opinions don't tell you much about a person because opinions change. Character's pretty consistent. How people make decisions is a part of their character.

Playing golf with a person, you find out what they're like under stress. You see how they deal with disappointment. You find out what they're like when they're thinking, deliberating. You see how long it takes for them to make a decision and whether they second-guess themselves. You get to see the whole person. When they win, do they gloat or are they gracious? Do they quit in frustration after seven strokes? Are they impulsive? Rational? Careful? Too careful? And most important, if they make the wrong decisions, how do they react? Are they good sports about it? Or do they pick up the ball and go home in a snit? Do they wrap their club around the tree when they miss a shot or when they hit over par? You need to know these things before hiring someone, partnering with them, handing them a franchise, a cheque or the reins of your company. And where else do you get a four-hour stretch to do that? I'll tell you something: I have never been wrong about someone I've played golf with.

Here's the thing I've come to believe about decisions: 99% of the time, my first decision is my best decision. The rest of the time I'm recalculating. It's like using a GPS system: Although the destination doesn't change, how I get there, the path I take, will always change. You start the car and plug in your address. The GPS can guide you to your destination, but it doesn't know about construction, detours, traffic jams and unexpected weather. At every such holdup, *you* have to make a decision. Go left or right? Keep going forward or turn the car around and backtrack? Pull over and wait out the storm? Just like with business, you're always recalculating. Your destination, your goal, the 18th hole, isn't going to change. But your route to get there does.

My job as an entrepreneur is to continually read the signs and symbols, and to make the million little decisions required to stay on course to reach my goal. Or perhaps I have to get off the course and change the destination entirely, like George and I did when Boston Pizza pulled out of Asia and Ontario and recalculated before re-entering successfully. The goal has never changed—to grow our company—but the route has changed drastically.

So I stand and deliberate on a golf course with the same concentration I use to figure out if a vacant lot on a street corner or an empty commercial space would make an ideal location for a franchise. I need to physically go there. I need to stand outside and get a feel for the location. I need to see and sense the place before making the crucial decision to set up a franchise there. I want to know, what's the foot traffic like here? Is there parking? Who is our competition? Which theatres, stadiums and high schools are nearby? Where's the closest highway? The closest airport? What's the key industry around here? The demographics? What was here before and why did it fail (or succeed)?

Why wasn't I a natural golfer? Because when I was a child, my dad taught me how to skate. A coach taught me how to play hockey. I learned how to throw a ball before I was taught how to ride a bike. But I picked up a golf club before I was taught how to play properly. I was well into middle age, set in my ways, before I finally decided to take my first lesson. And I have discovered something pretty crucial about myself, something that has contributed more to my success than almost anything else: I can still take direction.

A few years ago, I was at the Dallas National Golf Club. It was a Monday. I had a meeting with a local developer, and he suggested a morning game. I didn't know the guy, but he was angling for a big contract, and a round of golf would help me decide whether he was someone I wanted to do business with. We were on the tenth hole, a par three. I had never played the course before, but the developer was familiar with the hole and suggested a particular angle of approach.

"Jim, it's about 146 yards. Hit towards the tree. It should roll to the right."

He and the caddy went ahead to watch where my ball landed. I pulled out a Boston Pizza ball and balanced it on the tee. I picked a seven iron out of the bag and teed up, keeping his suggestion in mind. It was a humid, sticky day, a bit of a breeze behind me. I took a whack at the ball. I could feel right away it was a good swing. I watched the developer as he watched the ball arc across the sky, then disappear behind the knoll. A second later he threw his hands up.

"Jim! It's in!" he screamed.

A hole-in-one, my first and only one so far. What a great feeling! There is some luck involved in landing one. But luck is usually a result of a set of decisions that puts you in the right place to begin with. That's why I love to say that the harder I worked, the luckier I got. Mostly, I was willing to take the developer's direction: I listened to a man familiar with the course and the hole, and followed his advice. And by the way, he got the contract.

I was not taught how to be an entrepreneur. But I wanted to learn. From making sauce to structuring our finances, I wanted to get better all the time. Still do. Remember, I bought into the restaurant business before I knew how to run a restaurant. But let me tell you, I don't think there is any other way to do it—at least not for me. Learning about business in school does not make you a good decision maker, nor does it remove fear. In school, you can learn about economics, accounting and marketing. But until you're poring over a ledger at four in the morning trying to figure out how to make payroll, you don't really know anything about accounting.

Same with golf. I've studied the game, read about the game, watched pros play the game and practised the game on some incredible simulators. In the end, to improve my game and to eventually become really good at the game, I had to get out there and play the game. To do that, I had to be willing to be bad at it at first, to make mistakes and even to fail. I had to be willing to retreat at times and course-correct. I also had to keep on picking up that club and taking a swing. And then I had to miss. And miss again. Then I had to readjust at the next hole, and maybe decide on a different club. And after all that, I had to do the only thing left to do: take another swing.

ACKNOWLEDGEMENTS

As I've often said, the story of my life is really just a story of connections, each one bringing me to where I am today. So many people have been part of this story, I know I won't able to mention all of them in this book, let alone thank them individually. But when you're writing a book about a successful company that was built on good decisions, you have to thank folks like your first hockey coaches, so thank you: each of you shaped my early thinking about teamwork and decision making. I also feel a lot of gratitude for the people in my hometown, Virden, Manitoba, who gave me early guidance in life. But it all started with my parents, Ted and Mina Treliving. From them I learned to make real connections with people. They taught me everything I know about love, leadership and building partnerships. I owe them a lot, and I miss them. Love and thanks to my sisters, Joy and Pat, and their husbands, Guy and John, who have always been a great source of support and friendship. I want to extend a big thank you to Uncle Jack and Aunt Edna, who put me up at their place in Penticton all those years ago, making it possible for me to make a go of my very first venture. My daughter, Cheryl, my son, Brad, and his wife, Julie, have also been incredibly supportive and understanding all these years. It's tough having a dad always on the go. But my children have grown into the kind of adults I've come to admire, in no small part due to their mother, Elaine. Love and thanks also to my granddaughters, Candace and Samantha, Ryann and Reese. And I am a hell of a lucky guy to have met and married my wife, Sandi. She's helped me make some wise decisions in business and in life, and I consider her my biggest support, a key advisor, and my best friend. And her children, Katie and Dan, have been great companions on this ride.

A big thank you to all at HarperCollins Canada—you've all been incredible from the start in shaping the vision of this book and finding the right way for me to tell it—from Brad Wilson, my tireless and intuitive editor, and Jim Gifford, who saw this before any of us, to the crack editorial team, including Noelle Zitzer, Neil Erickson, Greg Tabor and Kelly Hope. I'm in the business of sales and marketing, and HarperCollins boasts the best team in the business, including Michael Guy-Haddock, Shelley Tangney, Cory Beatty, Charidy Johnston, Colleen Simpson and Rob Firing.

But my story is also the story of partnerships, starting with the amazing Agioritis brothers—Gus, George, Nino, Trifon and Perry—who opened the first Boston Pizza on August 12, 1964, in Edmonton. Many thanks to Don Spence, who took that first leap with me, and Ron Coyle, who handed us the reins. Big thanks to Bud and Ray Osborne, who provided me with the most interesting part-time gig; Mr. Dumpleton for that first loan; Duncan Meiklejohn from The Great Canadian River Race, for jogging my memory of that musical time in Penticton; and Bob Harris, my partner in Playmor Productions—boy, did we had fun. Much gratitude to Dave Gillespie and Bud Grant, without whom Boston Pizza would not be what it is or where it's at today. And thank you to Clement Ng, who introduced us to Asia, and Rick Arndt, who brought Boston Pizza into the 21st century: you're both a big part of our success, here and abroad.

Boston Pizza boasts some of the best business leaders in the world, including Mark Pacinda, who heads up our Canadian operations, and Mike Best, our man in America. I thank Bill Hancox, who moved his family from Canada to Texas and as head of operations continues to blend our Canadian Boston Pizza experience with Boston's in the US. Big thank yous also to Mike Cordoba, Mark Powell and Jordan Holm, who were among the brains behind the Boston Pizza Royalties Income Fund.

Despite the success of Boston Pizza, this book is really a by-product of my stint as a Dragon on CBC's *Dragons' Den*. For discovering me, I thank the inimitable CBC execs past and present: Tracie Tighe, Stuart Coxe, Julie Bristow, Jennifer Dettman and, of course, Kirsten Stewart. The show's senior producer, Lisa Gabriele, is a talented writer who not only put her stamp on a great TV show but has been utterly invaluable in helping me put this book together. A big thank you to her, and also to Rowan Anders, who's been my right-hand man for all of my *Dragons' Den* enterprises. Gratitude also to my fellow Dragons past and present: Arlene Dickinson, Kevin O'Leary, Robert Herjavec, Bruce Croxon, Brett Wilson, Jennifer Wood, Dave Chilton and the late great Laurence Lewin—we miss you, my friend. We share a lot more than a few partnerships in our Dragon enterprises, but this TV show, this experience, has been a hell of a ride.

Gratitude forever to my F-Troop mates of the RCMP, especially the unforgettable Barry Hughes. And thank you to Ted Ticknor, rest his soul—he was a good friend and great businessman. Finally, eternal thanks to George Melville, who has shared this journey and this story with me, and who helped me build my dream. I owe a big thank you also to his wife, Sylvia, who has been along for the ride with us. Each of you has contributed so much to this story, and you continue to help me write every beginning in my life. Thank you.

THE BOSTON PIZZA FOUNDATION

George Melville and I formed the Boston Pizza Charitable Foundation in 1990, and since then it has raised and donated more than $15 million. My daughter, Cheryl Treliving, became our executive director in 2008 and has continued our commitment to spearheading various fundraising initiatives, with the help of our franchisees and their staff from coast to coast. We've formed key relationships with the Heart & Stroke Foundation of Canada, JDRF (Juvenile Diabetes Research Foundation) and Kids Help Phone. And though we also give to a number of cancer foundations and the Canadian Red Cross, the charities that help children are the ones we focus on the most, including Big Brothers and Big Sisters, the Starlight Foundation and the Youth Emergency Shelter Society.

Our famous "heart-shaped pizza" campaign has raised almost $3 million for the Heart & Stroke Foundation, and we were moved give to JDRF because one of our own employees had a son stricken with Type 1 diabetes. We focus our funding for JDRF on one area in particular: the Clinical Islet Transplant Program at the University of Alberta, an experimental treatment for Type 1 diabetes, which could help the body make its own insulin and reduce the need for daily injections.

By the way, if you're a fan of *Dragons' Den*, you're helping too, because all the money I make on that program goes directly to several charities. Proceeds from this book will also go to various charities, such as the Centre for Addiction and Mental Health, which works tirelessly to remove the stigma of mental illness in this country. This gives "being a Dragon" purpose beyond just having my mug on TV or the cover of a book: I can drive a lot of attention to important causes. Because the real power of money is helping people. So if you want to give, or you'd like more information, please visit us online:

CANADA: www.bostonpizza.com/en/bp-foundation
U.S.: www.bostons.com/foundation
FACEBOOK: Boston Pizza Foundation
TWITTER: @BPIFoundation